MW00577440

REPO MAN

WRITTEN BY ALEX COX

PUBLISHED SCRIPT EDITED BY DICK RUDE

faber and faber
BOSTON · LONDON

NOT JUST A JOB —
IT'S AN ADVENTURE!

LOS ANGELES POLICE DEPARTMENT
VEHICLE REPOSSESSION REPORT

08.25.G (10-72)

DATE AND TIME REPOSSESSED

LOCATION WHERE VEHICL

ADDRESS

ADDRESS

Copyright © 1984 by Universal Pictures, a Division of
Universal City Studios, Inc. Reprinted by permission of
MCA Publishing Rights, a Division of MCA, Inc.
Introduction Copyright © 1987 by Alex Cox
and Dick Rude.

Library of Congress Cataloging-in-Publication Data
Cox, Alex.
Repo man / by Alex Cox ; edited by Dick Rude.
p.   cm.
ISBN 0-571-12977-3 (pbk.) : $9.95
I. Rude, Dick.   II. Repo man (Motion picture)   III.
Title.
PN1997.R46C6   1988   87-32979
791.43'72—dc19   CIP

Printed in the USA.

Book design by Boskydell Studio

DEDICATION
This book is for my parents.

ACKNOWLEDGMENTS
Various characters and the supermarket scene
were stolen from the screenplay *Leather
Rubbernecks,* written by Brant Reiter and Dick
Rude.
There would be no *Repo Man* without Mark
Lewis, Peter McCarthy, Jonathan Wacks, X,
Circle Jerks, Fear, Black Flag, Suicidal
Tendencies, Burning Sensations, Juicy
Bananas, Iggy Pop, and most of all Los
Plugz/Cruzados.
The photographs were taken by Martin
Turner. He and Jonathan Wacks wrote the
final scene.

HEALTH WARNING
Parts of this screenplay do not appear in the
finished film.

A REPO MAN SPEAKS OUT

Mark Lewis talks to Alex Cox and Dick Rude.

Alex: So the reason all this came about, the reason we are sitting here in Mark's backyard in Venice, California, is that Mark and Ed Pansullo were roommates.

Mark: Actually we encountered each other in the fabulous Camwood Apartments on Venice Boulevard and Beethoven in the year prior to 1977. Ed was an actor, of all things. My god, an actor. I couldn't believe it.

Alex: And I used to live over on Penmar and would drop by to see Ed and have a couple of brews.

Mark: Ed knew a lot of people.

Alex: He still does. And you were a repo man and thence began the saga. I was never a repo man, but I was your accomplice on a couple of jobs. My favorite was the day I got to drive the car.

Mark: You got to drive a Cadillac, no less. Out there in Studio City. The victim was a stockbroker with a history of non-payment, this being his second or third repo. I guess he was a three-time loser.

Alex: He was in the Presto Print getting his business cards.

Mark: I believe he was in the laundromat. We trailed him from his apartment and got him half way thru the wash cycle. He never knew what hit him, Al. The son of a bitch walked out with an armful of clean clothes and no trunk to put 'em in. And you had a hand in that. That wasn't nice the way you drove off in that red Cadillac.

7

Alex: I thought starting out what a terrible thing it was to be a repo man, what a wicked and immoral thing it was, but I really enjoyed stealing people's cars.

Mark: Absolutely. One of the first times I went out was with a fellow countryman of yours. He slim jimmed the car, got in, and found the driver's hat. It was a fairly expensive hat with a little feather in it. He walked over to a mud puddle, set it in the mud puddle, and jumped up and down on it three or four times. Then he picked it up and set it back in the car. That was my first lesson in dealing with personal properties. I later found that a lot of people who had their cars repossessed were slobs in their eating habits and would leave food in their cars. Fast food, you know. So I would always include the fast food remnants along with their personal property.

Alex: So this would be put in a bag, right?

Mark: Yes. All items in the car must be *properly* tagged and itemized. It's very important. This guy has just had his car repoed and is mad and naturally he wants his flashlight back. I received an official reprimand for including half-eaten sandwiches in property bags.

Alex: Which the victim would get several days later.

Mark: Sometimes several weeks later. However, it was brought to my attention down at one of the towing yards in a rather rough part of town, that the rats were attracted to the food, and were gnawing their way into the property bags, thusly destroying not only the personal property . . .

Alex: But the bag itself.

Mark: Yes, the lovely down bag that the property went into. Of course I was thoroughly lectured on the proper procedure of stowing away personal property and itemizing the things.

Dick: I'm sure you had a lot of dogs attack you in the line of duty.

Mark: I only got bit once. Animals are bad news. They can only be a problem. Sometimes they would actually be in the car. A guy I worked with got bit, tore a hole in his pants, and the company was so cheap they wouldn't fork over the money for a new pair of pants. So what if it's only fifteen bucks? It's the principle. You got your pants damaged in pursuit of your job, but no money comes towards the pants. That's how cheap the company was. A good repo man would not let a dog bother him in the least. I was always afraid of being in a car and getting shot while I was in the car. It's every repo man's nightmare because it's so real. It could happen any time. It don't have to be in the middle of the night. It could happen anywhere. And you could just hear the guy telling the judge, "Man this dude was stealing my car." You were on his property with a lock breaker. The guy gets a plea bargain and you know he's gonna get off or do twenty-four months of low security and you're dead.

Dick: What type of areas have the majority of repossessions?

Mark: I've spent time all over. In very nice areas as well as poor areas. Generally they're in the poor areas. The black and Mexican areas. But that didn't mean they had a monopoly on flakism. It was all over. Beverly Hills was a daily stop on my itinerary as well as Watts or Inglewood. You name it, I was there. I always made sure to keep this area clean of repo victims. I didn't want them giving Venice a worse name than it already had.

Alex: You were kind of like a volunteer policeman in a way.

Mark: Like a credit cop. I had to deal with people who elected, sometimes thru no fault of their own, and sometimes thru their own volition, not to pay. It was my responsibility to enforce the codes of the office. And that was to remove from them their car or to collect the payments current.

Alex: When you see a policeman, do you feel a warm feeling of brotherhood?

Mark: No, not really. But let me tell you, one time I got stopped for speeding in the pursuit of my beloved duties. And the officer said to me that I was crazy to do that stuff. He said that stuff's more dangerous than what he does. I never thought of it that way. In that respect I was a little crazy, because I was going down into some areas that even the cops will only go into in twos or threes, such as Nickerson Gardens, which is on Imperial down near Watts. The cops will never go in there by themselves. It's always at least two of them, and they have guns.

9

Alex: What did you think of the film we made in terms of its depiction of the repo life?

Mark: I thought it was fairly accurate. The one scene where Emilio jumps in the car and that guy comes around and starts choking him was very accurate. The slim jim, the lock breaker, the Christmas trees. Extremely accurate.

Alex: Was it true about the Christmas trees? That there was one in every repo car?

Mark: Well, I wouldn't say in every car, but I sure had a lot of them. I made it a practice to immediately yank them from the mirror and give them to my tow driver. He had a stack of a hundred of 'em, a foot wide, hanging from his emergency brake.

Alex: They're popular in Spain as well. In Southern Spain. Also in Scotland.

Mark: You're kidding. Christmas trees? I would never have believed it. I used to get sick of that stuff. To me, the Christmas tree was synonymous with a repossession. Like eighty-five percent of cars I ever repossessed had one. I mean, the cars reeked like shit. I hated that smell, like stale cherry perfume. There were so many of them I couldn't believe it. I thought that maybe there was a brotherhood of flakes out there that all liked Christmas trees. Then they started getting into the strawberries and the dice. They would all be air fresheners, but mostly it was Christmas trees.

Alex: The Christmas tree is definitely the most popular.

Mark: Oh, by far. It must be the most popular car item. They sell them at car washes, you know. So maybe people who get their cars washed might get a little Christmas tree.

Alex: They get a new tree and get all excited.

Mark: Yeah. Most of them have the money to buy little ornaments for their cars but they don't have money for their payments.

Alex: Yeah. The crooks.

Mark: They weren't all crooks, Al. There were some hard-working people who were trying. Four years is a long time to pay on a car.

Things happen. You work, you get fired from your job, you start school. I would walk into the office and immediately these big shots are coming down on me: "What do you know about this guy?" "Where's this guy's car?" "What do you know about these guys?" And I realized that I was the front line between this big corporation that has millions of dollars in outstanding loans, and the victims, who were ordinary people.

Alex: How did you leave the repo trade?

Mark: It was just bureaucracy, just putting up with big corporations and bosses that never spend any time out there in the field and can't relate to what you have to do all day. They wanted to put me behind a desk, farm the repossessions out to a cowboy outfit. When I declined, they wanted to know where the company car was. "Where's the car, Mark? Where's the car?" Think of how ironic it would be if I decided to make them repo their own company car. I declined their official ride home.

Alex: And you walked home?

Mark: Yeah. First I gave them the location of the car, then I cleaned out all my personal property, all my repo tools and my briefcase, and put them in one of those bags. Then I walked back to Venice. From the office, which was down near Vermont and Wilshire, along Wilshire and crossed down to Olympic, and down Barrington in west L.A., and then over to Gateway . . . that turns into Ocean Park, I think. I walked down around Santa Monica Airport, out toward here.

Alex: That's a long walk, Mark.

Mark: Yeah. I was giving a lot of thought to leaving the job. A lot of thoughts going thru my head that day, walking on down Wilshire. All for the best, though. It's a great feeling, seeing the repo car for the first time. Then you'll do almost anything to get it. You almost don't care if they come out, because unless they've got a gun or block you with another vehicle, you're gonna get that car. You got to meet a lot of interesting people and you got to see a lot of different places where people worked. It was very much a learning experience.

Alex: But in the end . . .

Mark: Ah, the futility of it all. There's no chance of winning. The amount of people never ends. There has gotta be something more worthwhile to life outside of money and momentary thrill. I mean, whaddya gonna do—spend the rest of your life searching out deadbeats?

Venice, California, USA
August 1987

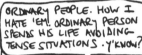

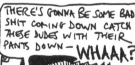

KEY: (A) RAY MAKES HARD LEFT TURN THRU CENTRAL DIVIDER; (B) SEVERAL SMALL IMPORTS COLLIDE & BURN; (C) PETERBILT REAR-ENDS PINTO; (D) RENTED BUS CONTAINING CHURCH CHOIR IS RUN OFF ROAD; (E) UNOBSERVANT COP.

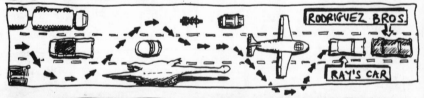

TO BE CONTINUED...

DESERT HIGHWAY. EXTERIOR. DAY

A MOTORCYCLE COP *lurks behind a billboard advertising Reverend Larry's Gospel Vigilante Hour. A Chevy Malibu approaches. It weaves back and forth across the center line. Unintelligible singing from the* DRIVER. *The Malibu passes in the wrong lane. The cop takes off with lights and sirens blazing. It is a long time before the driver notices and veers off the road . . .*

MALIBU. INTERIOR. DAY

J. FRANK *pulls up. The cop dismounts. J. Frank wears shades with one lens missing. His temples are cropped tight against his skull.*

> J. FRANK
> Bright light city gonna set my soul
> Gonna set my soul on fire . . .

The cop taps on the window. J. Frank winds it down.

> COP
> Let me see your driver's license.

J. Frank searches in his pocket. The cop frowns. Finally he indicates the license, lying beside J. Frank's wallet on the dash.

> COP
> Been drinking, sir?

19

Been driving long?
How far you headed?
You on some kinda medication?

> J. FRANK
Why, no. Do I seem "high"? I am high. High on life!

> COP
Uh huh. What you got in the trunk?

> J. FRANK
Oh . . . you don't want to look in there.

> COP
Give me the key.

Reluctantly, J. Frank detaches the trunk key. The cop takes it and walks around back. J. Frank watches in his rearview mirror. The trunk lock clicks.

A nosy cop (Varnum Honey) gets disintegrated.

HIGHWAY. EXTERIOR. SUNSET

The cop raises the trunk lid. A brilliant light pours forth. The cop hesitates, then raises the lid the rest of the way. The light intensifies. The cop screams and starts to disintegrate. We see his skeleton. Then it too disappears. The trunk falls shut. TILT DOWN *to his smoking boots. J. Frank puts the Malibu in gear and drives away.*

PIC'N'PAY. INTERIOR. NIGHT

OTTO *prices cans of spinach. His cheerful co-worker and hated adversary* KEVIN *neatly stacks the cans. They both wear badges that say HI! I'M—*
——! HERE TO SERVE! Commercial muzak.

> KEVIN
> Feelin' 7-Up, I'm feelin' 7-Up
> Sharin' smiles, sharin' styles,
> I'm feelin' 7-Up.

singing Marlboro theme?

Otto lowers the pricer. Stares at Kevin very hard.

> KEVIN
> It's a crisp refreshin' feelin',
> Crystal clear and light,
> Havin' fun with 7-Up
> And it sure feels right—

> OTTO
> Kevin, stop singing that!

> KEVIN
> What? I wasn't singing, guy.

Otto stamps Kevin's glasses with the pricer.

> OTTO
> Don't tell me you weren't singing. I'm standing right
> next to you and you were fucking singing. Cut it out.

KEVIN
Why so tense, guy?

Kevin backs away. Then he leaps to attention as MR. ASSISTANT MAN-
AGER HUMPHRIES *appears, flanked by an* ARMED GUARD.

MR. HUMPHRIES
Otto, you were late again today. Normally, I'd let it go
but it's been brought to my attention that you're not
paying attention to the spacing of the cans. The cans
must be placed equidistantly upon the shelves. The way
your young friend Kevin does it.

KEVIN
Maximizes Eye Appeal!

MR. HUMPHRIES
Exactly. I don't know if you realize how lucky you are
to have this lovely job, Otto. Most young men your
age in these uncertain times — Otto are you listening
to me?

OTTO
Fuck you.

MR. HUMPHRIES
Pardon?

*Otto hurls Kevin against a pyramid of cans. The cans collapse on Mr.
Humphries. The guard draws his gun. Otto lifts his hands and marches
silently toward the exit. Kevin titters.*

MR. HUMPHRIES
(to Kevin)
What are YOU laughing at? Luis, throw him out of here
too!

Strains of SLAMDANCE MUSIC *are heard . . .*

Otto (Emilio Estevez) and Kevin (Zander Schloss) get fired
by Mr. Humphries (Charles Hopkins) and the security guard (Luis Contreras).

STARWOOD PARKING LOT. EXTERIOR. NIGHT

The tuneful SOUNDS OF FEAR *pour forth from a tinny stereo. Otto dances
in the parking lot, colliding with his* PALS. *Girls stand on the sidelines,
shove the boys. The only thing missing is a band.*

> VOICES
> Fourth time in a row they cancelled. Maybe it's another
> night.

*Out of the evening mist, backlit by headlights, strides an epic figure in
a baggy suit.* DUKE. *Otto's age and mean. The other punkers eye Duke
warily. Duke eyes the delectable* DEBBI. *Then Otto sees him and grabs
his lapels —*

23

OTTO
How're ya doin' Duke? When did you get out of the
slammer, man?

Duke resists — then lets himself be dragged into the thrashing mini-throng.

BEDROOM. INTERIOR. NIGHT

*Otto and Debbi make out on Kevin's parents' queensize. Outside, a
scratchy record carries on the song. Otto prissily folds his trousers.*

OTTO
Excuse me while I fold my pants.

DEBBI
What's the difference?

OTTO
Nothing.

He lays back, cold as a fish.

DEBBI
Otto? Otto?

OTTO
What.

Debbi stares at the door.

DEBBI
Get me another beer.

KITCHEN. INTERIOR. NIGHT

Otto emerges from the bedroom. ARCHIE, *a spotty kid with a green mohawk, reels unsteadily into the bedroom after him. Otto heads for the
fridge. Kevin is rooting through the records. His hair is greased straight
up. Everyone else is stoned.*

KEVIN
I fucked 'er in the bathtub and the shower! I fucked 'er
in her parents' bed and on the pool table and on the
kitchen floor! Didn't bother with no birth control shit
neither!

*Otto takes a can marked BEER from the refrigerator. Duke proffers him
the bong.*

DUKE
What's happening?

Otto winks broadly, indicates the bedroom door.

BEDROOM. INTERIOR. NIGHT

Dark inside. Otto opens the door. MUFFLED SOUNDS *rise from the bed.*

OTTO
Debbi? I got your beer.

*No answer. Otto turns the lights on. Debbi and Archie are getting down.
She squints.*

DEBBI
Thanks, Otto. Leave it by the door.

ARCHIE
And put the fucking light out!

Otto leaves the light on, slams the door.

KITCHEN. INTERIOR. NIGHT

*Otto sits at the kitchen table with the stoners. He arm wrestles Duke over
broken bottles.*

KEVIN
We lost our jobs today! Cause we was punkers! Right, Otto? I got so mad I pissed in the Community Pool!

OTTO
So, uh, how was it in Juvy, Duke? I always meant to come and visit you, you know.

DUKE
Thanks, Otto.

OTTO
No man, I really did. I don't know why I never got around to it. Fuckin' Pic'N'Pay I guess. You staying with your folks?

DUKE
They threw me out. Where can I get a gun?

Otto frowns. Out of the corner of his eye Duke sees Archie emerging from the bedroom. Duke rises.

KEVIN
You gonna get a piece, Duke? Think I might get one too. .357 Python Grande, man, it makes a hole THIS BIG —wanna go in on it with me, Otto?

OTTO
(thrusting bong at Kevin)
Suck on this.

KEVIN
I don't get stoned anymore.

OTTO
Yes you do.

Archie opens the refrigerator. Otto sees him.

OTTO
You finished in there?

ARCHIE
She's all yours.

Archie makes squelching noises with his tongue.

BEDROOM. INTERIOR. NIGHT

Otto enters with another beer. Kevin tags behind him.

OTTO
Debbi, honey . . . I got your beer.

Hearing nothing, he turns on the lights. Duke is making love to Debbi.

DEBBI
Ignore him, Duke. He's nothing but a big baby.

KEVIN
What're you doin' man? Nobody's supposed to be here.

DUKE
. . . and turn out the fucking light.

KEVIN
This is my parents' room.

Otto grabs Kevin and throws him down the stairs.

STREET. EXTERIOR. DAWN

Otto staggers past factory walls. He has no destination. He carries five beers.

OTTO
(singing)
We got nothin' better to do
Than watch TV, have a couple of brews—

Otto sits down on the corner. The sky starts to light up.

OTTO
We're gonna have a TV party tonight
All right!
We're gonna have a TV party all right
Tonight!
Don't care about anyone else
We don't wanna know
We're gonna watch
Our favorite shows
SATURDAY NIGHT LIVE!
MONDAY NIGHT FOOTBALL!
JEFFERSONS!
DALLAS!
GILLIGAN'S ISLAND!
FLINTSTONES!—

A Chevy Malibu rolls up the street toward us. It passes Otto in slow motion. It has New Mexico plates.

ALLEY. EXTERIOR. MORNING

Otto kicks a can up the back street. He passes a beat-up Chevy Impala. Behind the wheel sits BUD, *reading* All Sports. *Bud is maybe forty-five. Tough and tired, nervous yet nonchalant. Chainsmokes Commanders.*

MARLENE (V.O.)
(via CB)
—also be on the lookout for a '67 Chevy Malibu from out
of state. Collateral one thousand dollars—

BUD
Hey, kid!

Otto doesn't hear him. Bud rolls after Otto.

BUD
Hard of hearing, Ace?

OTTO
What do you want?

BUD
You wanna make ten bucks?

OTTO
Fuck you, queer.

BUD
You got the wrong idea, son. Smoke Commanders?

OTTO
Of course.

BUD
Have one of mine. See my old lady's real sick. I've got
to get her to the hospital.

OTTO
So, take her there.

BUD
And leave my other car behind? This is a BAD
NEIGHBORHOOD. I need some helpful soul to drive it
for me. So I can get momma to the hospital. She's
pregnant, see. With twins. Could drop at any time.

OTTO
How much you gonna give me?

BUD
Fifteen bucks.

29

OTTO
Won't do it for less than twenty.

BUD
Twenty-five.

Otto is taken aback. Bud jangles the car keys.

BUD
You follow me in my old lady's car. It isn't far.

OTTO
(accepting keys)
Okay. Where's your old lady at?

BUD
We'll get her on the way. Right now the most important
thing is to get both my vehicles out of this BAD AREA.
Right?

Bud indicates a nearby Cutlass Supreme. Otto opens the door.

CUTLASS. INTERIOR. DAY

*Otto adjusts the seat. He turns the radio on, starts hunting for a station.
Bud guns the Impala motor.*

RADIO VOICES
—make money for doing nothing—
—voted to expand the war in Guatemala—
—Christmas five weeks earlier this year—
—pork futures after this—

*Bud hits the horn impatiently. Otto ignores him. TWO OLD PEOPLE emerge
from an adjacent house. They point at the Cutlass. Bud takes off up the
street.*

ALLEY. EXTERIOR. DAY

The old man grabs the door handle. The old lady hurls her rosary after the car. It catches on the fender and drags in the dirt. Bud turns a corner. Otto does the same.

CUTLASS. INTERIOR. DAY

Otto looks behind. He is not pursued. A diabolical grin spreads across his face.

FREEZE FRAME. *Unfold the dread words:*

CUTLASS. INTERIOR. DAY

Otto slows as the Impala halts before a cyclone fence. An unkempt character, MILLER, *opens the gates. Otto follows Bud into the*

REPO YARD. EXTERIOR. DAY

Miller locks the gate again. He drags an oily drum across the yard. The drum is labelled "PERSONAL AFFECTS." Bud jumps out of the Impala and hurries up the office steps. Otto gets out of the Cutlass. He watches Miller drag personal belongings from the car. LITE, *a handsome repo operative, sits in the front seat of a wreck, combing his hair. Funk music. He ignores Otto's stare. Otto follows Bud up the stairs.*

OLY'S VOICE
Don't have it. Try another yard.

MINER'S VOICE
You think I don't know my own car, mister? It's sitting right outside.

REPO OFFICE. INTERIOR. DAY

Bud freezes in the doorway. OLY, *master of the repo yard, toys with a set of car keys. Opposite him stands* MINER, *an angry man who lifts a lot of weights. Miner is with his girlfriend,* DELILAH. PLETTSCHNER, *a cowardly cop, lurks by the coffee urn.* MARLENE, *a gorgeous unapproachable receptionist, talks on the phone.*

MARLENE
Helping Hand Acceptance Corporation, Marlene speaking.

MINER
. . . it took me two weeks to get this money up so I could come and get it.

OLY
That ain't your car.

DELILAH
Hey, you gonna let him lie to you like that?

MINER
Shut up. Shut up.

DELILAH
Huh?

MINER
You gonna give me my car or do I gotta go to your house and shove your dog's head down the toilet?

PLETTSCHNER
Take it easy, sonny boy.

DELILAH
Shut up, rent-a-cop.

OLY
Best goddamned car on the lot.

MINER
Damn right it is.

Oly grabs Miner's money. Miner grabs his keys. They eye each other murderously. Then both men burst out laughing. Miner leads Delilah out the door.

PLETTSCHNER
Live in a Cadillac, sleep in a tent.

Plettschner looks for approval. He gets none.

BUD
Shut up, Plettschner.

MARLENE
(into phone)
Helping Hand Acceptance Corporation, Marlene speaking . . .

BUD
I'm all out of contract driver forms, Oly. Gimme one of yours.

OLY
Sure, Bud. Gimme a buck.

MARLENE
(studying Bud's paperwork)
LAPD? I want to report a repo in the West Palms district. What street was the car on, Bud?

BUD
Some alley. Hey, punk—
(*as Otto enters*)
—what street was the Cutlass on?

OTTO
I don't know. Where's your old lady?

BUD
Shit! I forgot all about her. She can ride the bus. She's a
rock. Marlene, Oly, this here is my new contract driver.
Got a name?

OTTO
Otto.

OLY
AUTO? AUTO PARTS! AHAHAHAHAH!

Oly tosses Otto a beer. The phone rings. Oly picks it up.

OLY	MARLENE
Helping Hand . . .	You got a driver's
Whaahuh? Oh YEAH?	license, sonny? Let me
You're fuckin' 'A' we	see it.
ripped your car,	(*Otto hands it to her*)
ASSHOLE! Wanna	Are you really twenty-
know who told us where	one?
it was? YOUR	
GODDAMNED	OTTO
BROTHER!	It says so, doesn't it?

Oly slams the phone down. Gives Otto his sweetest smile.

OLY
Need some help with that beer?

OTTO
You're all . . . REPO MEN.

34

Otto.
"You're all Repo Men."

OLY
What if we are?

Otto pops his beer open. Pours it on the floor.

BUD
Kid. When I see someone looks the way you do, my first
reaction is, I want to smash his face in. But you know
what?
(in unison with Oly)
YOU'RE ALL RIGHT!

35

Lite enters. He ignores Bud. Goes to his desk and rifles through the papers piled upon it.

BUD
Right, Lite?

LITE
(ignoring him)
You got any messages for me, baby?

MARLENE
Here you go.

OLY
Cracks me up.

LITE
Somebody piss on the floor again?

Otto grabs the door handle. Oly pushes a button. The door locks automatically.

OLY
Where you goin', kid? Have another beer! Maybe he's looking for a job, hey Budski?

BUD
Could be. We're always on the lookout for a few good men.

OTTO
Screw that! Ain't gonna be no REPO MAN! No way!

MARLENE
It's too late. You already are.

She fans out five crispy new fives. Otto grabs them. The door clicks open. Otto jams out, followed by a shower of beer.

REPO YARD. EXTERIOR. DAY

Miller removes things from the Cutlass, drops them in his drum. He beckons to Otto, holding out a little blue Christmas tree in-car air freshener.

> MILLER
> Find one in every car. You'll see.

Miller presses the Christmas tree into Otto's hand. He grins. He has no teeth. Otto dashes out the gate.

DESERT HIGHWAY. EXTERIOR. DAY

A similar blue Christmas tree hangs from the windshield of the late policeman's motorcycle, abandoned at the side of the road.

PULL FOCUS *thru the windshield to the desert, where* FIGURES IN ALL-OVER FALLOUT SUITS *search for pieces of the cop. One of them holds up a charred arm! Buzzards cackle.*

> FIGURE
> Look! Another bit!

AGENT ROGERSZ *walks toward her van. She is blonde, attired like a school-mistress. Her van is boxlike and anonymous. Police car alongside. The* SHERIFF *shakes his head. She gets into the van.*

> SHERIFF
> Never seen the like of it. What could have done that to him? Gasoline? NAPALM?

> AGENT ROGERSZ
> It happens sometimes. People just explode. Natural causes.

She slams the door.

VIDEO VAN. INTERIOR. DAY

Darkness within. Lights flicker on. High tech video consoles featuring maps and figures. Agents Rogersz pushes buttons. Words appear on a screen:

> PER/NSA/U232   SUSPECT PRESENCE
> ON WEST COAST CONFIRMED.   44% POSS.
> LOS ANGELES.   LOCATE IMMEDIATELY.
> *DO NOT NOTIFY POLICE.*

UNEMPLOYMENT OFFICE. EXTERIOR. DAY

Otto sits on the sidewalk. It is raining. CUTE SPANISH GIRLS *pass by giving him the eye. Kevin emerges with a sheaf of papers in his arms. He squats next to Otto.*

> OTTO
> *(reading Kevin's papers)*
> Night watchman, Pomona.

> KEVIN
> Yep.

> OTTO
> Asbestos worker, City of Industry.

> KEVIN
> Yep. Yep.

> OTTO
> French fry maker, Agoura. *(laughs)* That's absurd.

> KEVIN
> Yeah, well, you think that's funny, huh. There's fucking room to move as a fry cook, man. You know I could be manager in two years. King. God.

OTTO

You know, Kevin. I had this wild fucking dream the
other night.

KEVIN

I'll bet.

OTTO

It was with you and me and . . . we were working in
this sleazy shit-hole motel down in Miami, Florida, and
we were bell-hops and we were sixty-five years old. It
was so real, it was really, it was real, it was realistic, you
know?

KEVIN

And then what? You woke up in a puddle?

OTTO

(departing)

Fuck you, you fucking jerk.

KEVIN

Where you goin' asshole?

OTTO

Away from you.

OTTO'S PARENTS' HOUSE. EXTERIOR. DUSK

*Otto gets down off a smoking bus. He crosses the street to a walled,
grafittied bunker. Rattle of many keys.*

OTTO'S PARENTS' HOUSE. INTERIOR. NIGHT

Otto lets himself in. The drapes are drawn. Dust is everywhere. HIS
PARENTS *are hunched on the sofa. They wear pastel robes. They stare at*
REVEREND LARRY, *a TV evangelist, on the video screen.*

REV. LARRY
The Lord has told me personally, yea! For I walk with
the Lord, Amen! Larry, he said, you and your flock
shall see the PROMISED LAND! But only if you first
destroy the TWIN ABOMINATIONS of Godless
Communism abroad and Liberal Humanism at home!
Joyous Hallelujah! SMASH 'EM DOWN!

OTTO
Hi mom, hi dad. Anything to eat?

His parents' eyes remain glued to the screen. Otto finds something in the
kitchen zone. Generic can marked FOOD. He sits down, spooning from
it.

MOM
Put it on a plate, son. You'll enjoy it more.

OTTO
Couldn't enjoy it more, mom. Mmm mmm MMM! Dad.
Hey, dad.

DAD
What is it, son?

OTTO
Remember how you said one time you'd give me like a
thousand bucks to go to Europe if I finished school?
Well, sir, you were right! I really think I wanna do that
—finish school I mean—so can I have the money first?
Like, NOW? I really love you, dad. Mom too. DAD!

DAD
(*mumbling*)
I don't have it any more.

OTTO
What?

MOM
Your dad gave all our extra money to the Reverend's
Telethon. We're sending Bibles to El Salvador.

OTTO
But. What about me?

DAD
You're on the Chariots of Fire Honor Roll the same as
all of us, Otto. It was a gift from all of us, jointly.

The door slams sepulchrally.

REV. LARRY
(on TV)
Give me your money, NOW!

GARAGE. INTERIOR. DAY

*Otto beds down between his parents' third and second cars. The cars are
up on blocks. He lights a joint.*

REV. LARRY
(thru the wall)
I see . . . a sickly child, that's weakly and in pain! MY
FRIENDS! Bring forth that sickly little one and press
him 'gainst my healing hands. YEA! PRESS YOUR
BABY'S HEAD AGAINST THE BLESSED
TELEVISION SCREEN!

*Otto finishes the joint. He puts his Walkman headphones on, turns up
the volume, "Burning Down the House." Otto puts the light out, goes
to sleep.*

IMPALA. INTERIOR. DAY

*Otto sits next to Bud in the Repomobile. Scraps of paper, carbons,
cigarettes are scattered on the dashboard, jammed behind the shades.*

41

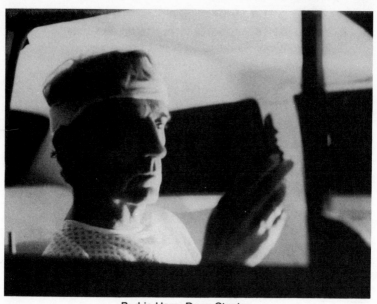

Bud is Harry Dean Stanton.
"Only an asshole gets killed for a car."

OTTO
How much do I get paid?

BUD
You don't get paid. You get Commission. That's better
than being paid. Most cars you rip are worth two or
three hundred bucks. Fifty thousand dollar Porsche
might make you five grand . . .

Bud honks at another driver.

BUD
C'mon, dickhead!

IMPALA. INTERIOR. NIGHT

Bud still drives. Otto sits alongside.

BUD
Keep your doors locked at all times. Ripping people's
cars can take you into some bad neighborhoods. It helps
if you dress like a detective. Detectives, they dress fairly
square. If people think, "This guy's a cop," they're
gonna think you're packing something. That way they
won't fuck with you so much.

OTTO
And are you?

What it's like to
be a missile man --
-- into it -

BUD
Am I what?

OTTO
Packing something.

BUD
Only an asshole gets killed for a car.

IMPALA. INTERIOR. DAY

Otto lights two Commanders, passes one to Bud. He scans the Thomas
Bros. Map. His dress has begun a slow process of evolution into detec-
tivehood.

BUD
Ripping somebody the first time's easy cause they don't
expect it. If they get their car back, they get smart.
Henceforth, they're gonna stash it somewhere, leave it
with a friend. Sometimes you drive around for days.
Sound interesting?

OTTO
Sounds better than Juvy. Turn left here.

BUD
Juvy? You just come out of Juvenile? What was you in
for, Ace?

43

OTTO

I don't like to be called Ace. Right at the light.

BUD

It wasn't MURDER, was it? I don't mind cons, but I
don't ride with murderers. Makes me uncomfortable.
Junkies too. Junkies won't hustle in this game. The guys
that make it are the ones that'll get in their car at any
time. Get home at three A.M., get up at four. There ain't
a repo man I know that don't take speed.

OTTO

Oh yeah? I got a friend that's selling real fine meth. It's
pharmaceutical!

BUD

Ain't no other kind.

PHONE BOOTH. EXTERIOR. DUSK

Otto makes like a detective. Bud shouts into the phone.

BUD

I don't believe you, Dolores! If you sent us a money
order, you can show me a RECEIPT! It's that or else
I'm gonna come and take your little Toyota away just
like the last time—HELLO?

*The phone is dead. He slams it down and picks it up again. Inserts
another dime. Nothing. Another dime. Nothing.*

BUD

FUCKING GENERAL TELEPHONE!

*Bud pulls a tire iron from the rear seat of the Impala. He smashes the
phone. Otto joins in enthusiastically.*

BUD

Let's go see your friend.

IMPALA. INTERIOR. NIGHT

Outside, TWO HANDSOME PEOPLE *in pristine tennis whites argue with Lite and the* TOW TRUCK DRIVER. *A Rabbit convertible hangs from the hooks. Lite and the tow truck driver laugh.*

PULL FOCUS *to Otto and Bud snorting lines of crank off the glove compartment door.*

> BUD
> *(tears rolling down his cheeks)*
> I never broke into a car. I never monkeyed with the wiring of a car. I never broke into a trunk. I shall not cause harm to any vehicle nor the personal contents thereof, nor through inaction let that vehicle or the personal contents thereof come to harm. It's what I call the Repo Code, kid. *(sniff)* Don't forget it. Etch it in your brain. *(sniff)* Not many people got a code to live by anymore.
> *(indicating Tennis Whites)*
> Look. Look at that. Look at those assholes over there.
> *(Tennis Man yells at Lite, egged on by Tennis Woman)*
> Ordinary people, how I hate 'em.

> OTTO
> *(eyes streaming)*
> Me too, I hate 'em too.

> BUD
> What do you know. Ordinary person spends his life avoiding tense situations. Repo Man spends his life getting into 'em. Let's go get a drink.

LIQUOR STORE. INTERIOR. NIGHT

Four white generic cans marked DRINK land on the counter. Otto digs in his pockets. Bud waves Otto's offering aside.

BUD

Tense situations. When you get into five or six of 'em a
day, gets to the point where it don't mean shit. I've seen
men stabbed. Didn't mean shit. Guns don't mean shit
either. That's when you got to watch yourself.

Bud pays for the drinks.

BUD

Here, I'll handle it pal. Settle down.

He picks up the purchase.

BUD

Have a nice day. I mean night. Day, night, doesn't mean
shit.

*Bud and Otto exit the store. Duke, Debbi, and Archie emerge from behind
the counter. They rob the till while holding the* STOREKEEPER *at gunpoint.*

DUKE

Wasn't that Otto?

DEBBI

Otto who?

HIGHWAY BRIDGE. EXTERIOR. NIGHT

The Malibu passes the van, stalled on the road. MEN IN WHITE FALLOUT
SUITS *are looking at the engine.*

UPTOWN STREET. EXTERIOR. DAY

Bud and Otto watch as a Mercedes is shackled to the tow truck.

BUD

If it's a new car you can get the keys off of the dealer.
Otherwise you have to call the truck. It's heartbreaking

to be sitting waiting for the truck and see the dildo come out of his house and drive away. But once you got that baby hanging from the hooks, she's yours!

MR. PAKMAN *comes running from his house. He wears a full-length robe and slippers.*

PAKMAN
I know my rights! There's no way you're gonna take this car! Absolutely no way!

BUD
(consulting clipboard)
Are you Miss Lu-Ann Pakman?

PAKMAN
Why—obviously not. My name is Arthur Pakman. Lu-Ann is my daughter. You'll have to take this matter up with her.

BUD
Don't think I haven't tried. She hasn't had the decency to contact us in months. I've been skip-tracing on this car all over town.

PAKMAN
My daughter has been sick. The damn car isn't running anyway. I'm sure that's why she hasn't paid you.

BUD
She could have called and told us. All I can say to you is call my branch manager. I'll abide by what he says.

Bud hands Pakman a card. Pakman studies it.

PAKMAN
"I.G. Farben"? What is this? You think I'm a moron? If I go inside you're going to tow my car away.

47

BUD
I'm not going to do that, sir. I'm going to wait right
here until you've spoken to him.

*Pakman extends a hand. Bud shakes it. Pakman goes into the house.
Bud signals to the driver, jumps in the Impala. He takes off down the
street with Otto running after him—*

L.A. RIVER. EXTERIOR. DAY

*The Impala pours out of darkness onto the caked-mud-concrete riverbed.
Bud guns the Impala upstream.*

IMPALA. INTERIOR. DAY

OTTO
Where are we going?

BUD
(lighting a Commander)
Gonna be some bad shit coming down one of these days.
Catch all these dildoes with their pants down.

OTTO
The Christians or the communists?

BUD
Whole fucking lot of 'em. You too. Freeways gridlocked,
airports grounded, Marina faggots fighting for the last
boat out. Thirty seconds till the end of everything.

OTTO
Where you gonna be then—on the moon?

BUD
Right here. Heading north at 110 per.

OTTO
You'll kill your car.

BUD
I only have to do it once! I got my spot picked out. I got
my supplies, a place I can hole up in when the shit
comes down . . .

*Otto yawns and looks the other way. He spies a black Falcon convertible
pacing them.*

OTTO
Cool car.

BUD
Uh oh. The Rodriguez Brothers.

OTTO
The motherfuckers flipped you off.

The Rodriguez Brothers, Lagarto (Del Zamora) and Napo (Eddie Velez).

49

BUD
Roll the window down. Roll the window down.

L.A. RIVER. EXTERIOR. DAY

Bud shouts unintelligibly at the Falcon's occupants. One of them waves to him. The other flips him off. Bud accelerates. The Falcon does too.

OTTO
Holy shit.

IMPALA. INTERIOR. DAY

Bud slams the car into a hard U-turn. It slithers up the bank and stalls. Bud and Otto get out. Otto is laughing.

BUD
Goddamned dip shit Rodriguez. Gypsy dildo. Punks! I'll get your ass.

OTTO
Wow. That was intense.

BUD
Repo Man's always intense. Come on, let's go get a drink.

OTTO
Gee, Bud, you never told me it was gonna be like this, man. Cops and robbers, real-life car chases . . .

LIQUOR STORE. INTERIOR. DAY

Duke backs toward the door. Archie holds it open. Debbi is the last to leave. She shoots the light out.

ARCHIE
Duke!

DUKE
You say our names we're gonna have to kill these
people, Archie!

ARCHIE
They all ran away.

DEBBI
Come on, you douche bags.

They run out. Archie runs into a concrete pole. Bud and Otto enter.

BUD
Awfully quiet in here. Too quiet.

IMPALA. EXTERIOR. DAY

OTTO
So who are these Rodriguez Boys?

BUD
The Rodriguez BROTHERS. Lagarto and Napoleon.
Two notorious delinquents currently responsible for at
least thirty vehicles in the field.

OTTO
How'd they manage that?

CAL WORTHINGTON. EXTERIOR. DAY

*The RODRIGUEZ BROTHERS are seen talking to CAL. They act deferential
and attentive. Cal extolls the virtues of a dead Vega. "A CHAL-
LENGE AT $99.99"*

BUD (V.O.)
What they do is this. One of them buys a hundred-dollar
junker and they pay it off on time. Never miss a
payment. Now they got a perfect credit record. Dig?

Rodriguez Brothers again talking to Cal. This time they are studying a gleaming row of top-of-the-line sedans.

>   BUD (V.O.)
> A week later they're back looking for another car. They
> sign the papers and they're outta there in a brand new
> Le Baron. No money down, and that's the last they ever
> see of 'em.

<u>CAMARO</u>. INTERIOR. DAY

Lite and Otto pull up alongside a convertible driven by MISS MAGRUDER.

>   OTTO
> Scumbags.

>   LITE
> They ain't scumbags. They're car thieves just like us.

>   LITE
> There's Miss Magruder. You wanna go for it?

Lite hands Otto a bag.

>   OTTO
> Good gag. You pull this one a lot?

>   LITE
> Only on the women. It never fails.

Otto gets out of the car and steps in front of the convertible.

>   OTTO
> Excuse me. Miss Magruder. I have something here for
> you.

Otto drops a dead rat into her car.

MISS MAGRUDER
Mmm. How utterly charming.

She sprays Otto with mace. The light changes. She drives away. Lite takes off after her. Blind Otto staggers around.

REPO OFFICE. INTERIOR. NIGHT

Marlene sits at the computer terminal, talking into the CB. Behind her, Oly watches nude aerobics on the TV screen.

OLY
Izzat right, asshole? Well, why dontcha! COME ON BY!
I'll be here waiting for ya—with a 12-gauge!

MARLENE
(into CB)
This is the ScanCar Repo Update for the evening of the 25th. Collateral on car number 228, a Chevy Malibu, has been raised from one thousand dollars to five thousand—

IMPALA. INTERIOR. NIGHT

Bud and Otto exchange an appreciative glance. The Impala surges forward out of frame.

LAUNDROMAT. EXTERIOR. DAY

The Impala reappears from the opposite direction. It screeches to a halt. PEASON, *an aggressive business type, pulls dirty washing from his Cadillac. His wash consists entirely of alligator shirts. He enters the laundromat.*

BUD
Bruce I. Peason. Brokerage consultant. Fuckin'
millionaire. Six payments behind. I've never understood
it.

OTTO
What's that?

BUD
Fuckin' millionaires. They never pay their bills. See you at the yard.

OTTO
Let me get this one.

BUD
No, I'll handle this one. Mr. Peason's carrying a permit for a pistol.

Otto takes the keys.

BUD
Hey, hey, hey. Give me that.

OTTO
Don't underestimate me, Ace.

Otto gets out of car, gets into the Cadillac parked there.

LAUNDROMAT. INTERIOR. DAY

Peason is engaged in heated dialogue with the CLIENTELE. *Outside, unnoticed, Otto gets into his car.*

PEASON
Look, it's very simple. I have three loads of washing so I need three machines. Naturally I want them to be next to one another. I also want them to be near the window so that I can watch them while I'm sitting in my car. All you have to do is take your washing out of this machine and put it in one of those others over there —

Otto drives Peason's Cadillac away. Laughter. Peason throws his coat-tail back so they can see his gun. More laughter. His holster is empty.

PEASON
My gun! Who took my gun!

CUSTOMER
Same person took your car.

CADILLAC. INTERIOR. DAY

Otto experiments with the electric windows and the digital displays. The interior is grungy and the plastic trim hangs loose. Blue Christmas tree air freshener on the dash. Suddenly Otto sees something moving fast along the sidewalk — LEILA, running with a bundle of maps under her arms. He buzzes the window down.

STREET. EXTERIOR. DAY

Otto paces Leila. She ignores him. He hits the horn.

OTTO
Hey, hey, you wanna ride?
Hey, baby, you need a ride?

He runs into some garbage cans. An OLD ENGLISH LADY appears waving a broom.

OLD LADY
Pick it up.

SONG ON RADIO
Pablo Picasso never got called an asshole!

Otto gets out of the car, kicks one of the cans.

OTTO
Huh?

OLD LADY
Look at you. You pick it up. You know yourself you were wrong.

OTTO
What were they doing out in the middle of the street?

OLD LADY
They weren't in the middle of the street. That's not the middle of the street. That's the corner. Go on, you pick it up.

OTTO
What?

OLD LADY
You pick it up. You knocked it over.

OTTO
(to Leila, as old lady talks)
Hey, you still want a ride, or what?

OLD LADY
No, I don't.

Otto and Leila get in the Cadillac and drive off.

SONG ON RADIO
Subsequently, Pablo Picasso was never called an asshole.

CADILLAC. INTERIOR. DAY

Otto lights two Commanders, offers Leila one. She shakes her head. He puts it, lit, behind his ear.

OTTO
My name's Otto.

LEILA
Leila. Is this your car?

OTTO
Yeah, it's one of them.

LEILA
One of them. Think you're pretty slick, don't ya? I bet
you're a used car salesman.

OTTO
I am not.

LEILA
You dress like one.

OTTO
I'm a repo man.

LEILA
What's that?

OTTO
It's a repossessor. I take back cars from dildoes who
don't pay their bills. Cool, huh?

LEILA
No.

*Leila gives him a dirty look. Then suddenly she dives beneath the dash-
board.*

OTTO
Uh . . . what are you doing?

LEILA
Those men in the car next to us. OTTO DON'T LOOK
AT THEM! If they see me they'll kill me.

Otto glances at the MEN. *Blond and blue-suited, driving an AMC Matador.*

OTTO
Oh really? Why—
(the cigarette burns his ear)
AAAAAARRRRGGGGHHH!!!

57

Otto slaps wildly at the Commander. The blond men glance over in surprise. Leila grabs the wheel and yanks it.

STREET. EXTERIOR. DAY

The Cadillac veers hard right across waste ground into an alley—up another alley—no one in pursuit.

CADILLAC. INTERIOR. DAY

Leila tries to look back. Otto pushes her head down.

>   OTTO
> Stay low. It looks like you were right. What's going on?

>   LEILA
> Take a look at this.

From her backpack she produces a crumpled photograph. Otto studies it, accelerating.

>   OTTO
> It looks like . . . sausage.

>   LEILA
> It isn't sausage, Otto. This is a photograph of FOUR
> DEAD ALIENS. Their UFO came down in 1947 in a
> lightning storm. The Government kept them on ice for
> thirty years—

>   OTTO
> Huh huh huh.

>   LEILA
> Laugh away, fuckface. This picture's gonna be in
> EVERY MAJOR NEWSPAPER in TWO DAYS'
> TIME.

>   OTTO
> How do you know?

LEILA
Promise not to tell? I'm in a secret network. This scientist who's also in our secret sect smuggled the corpses off this Air Force base. Now they've got them in the TRUNK OF HIS CAR. A Chevy Malibu. We've got to find him.

OTTO
And what are you going to do with 'em? Put 'em on Johnny Carson?

LEILA
Yes! We're going to hold a press conference and tell the world!

Otto bursts out laughing. Leila spies Peason's Magnum under the seat. She grabs it, points it out the window. Otto pushes buttons, jamming the window on her hand.

OTTO
We lost 'em. Put it DOWN!

ALLEY. EXTERIOR. DAY

The Cadillac weaves up the alley, skidding and hitting garbage cans. No one pursues them. It disappears.

UFO HEADQUARTERS. EXTERIOR. DAY

They pull up in front of the building and park.

OTTO
(*reading the sign on the wall*)
United Fruitcake Outlet?

LEILA
My door doesn't work.

Otto opens Leila's door. She emerges. They stare at each other dumbly.

59

LEILA
Thanks for the ride.

OTTO
Sure. Uh . . . I don't know. What do you think? Do you
want to go out with me again sometime?

LEILA
I don't know. I'm gonna kind of be busy with work.
And the Malibu and everything.

OTTO
Okay, great. Terrific. Here's your shit.

LEILA
What's your problem? I mean, girls might like you if
you lightened up a little bit.

OTTO
Fuck that! Girls pay to go out with me, alright?

LEILA
Wanna get back in the car?

OTTO
What, here?

*Otto nods. He and Leila dive into the back seat. The windows steam.
Giggles and squeals are heard.* TWO BEAMING PEOPLE *pass them, wearing
Happy Face badges. They enter the building.*

REPO OFFICE. INTERIOR. DAY

*Oly and Marlene stare at the computer monitor. Printout. They talk in
whispers. Miller whistling outside.*

OLY
Twenty thousand dollars for a CHEVY MALIBU? It's
got to be a joke. Who's putting up the money?

MARLENE
Double X Finance of Los Alamos. Storefront operation.
Money's in escrow.

Otto enters, jingling Cadillac keys. Oly crumples up the printout.

MARLENE
Want me to notify the boys?

OLY
Ah, no. They're always bitching 'bout their caseload.
I'm going out for a while.

MARLENE
Why, are we out of beer?

OLY
Somebody has to work around here.

*Oly goes to the refrigerator. Removes a pork pie hat. Otto picks up the
Weekly World News from a desk. It bears the headline, "E.T.S
WILL LAND ANY DAY NOW." The sausage photograph is under-
neath.*

Oly dons pork pie hat and heads for the door.

OLY
Keep making me money, kid.

OTTO
Fuck you.

CITY STREET. EXTERIOR. DAY

Lite and Otto approach a Camaro.

LITE
Man, we've been lookin' for this red devil for a long
time. Just act natural. Nobody knows if it's your car or

somebody else's car . . . Don't worry about that. (*hands Otto the slim jim*) Here, you give it a try, all right.

Otto opens the door and an alarm goes off. He gets in the other side. Lite attaches a wrench to the ignition. Otto watches, fascinated.

LITE
Put your seatbelt on. I never ride with anyone unless they wear their seatbelt. That's one of my rules.

Otto buckles his belt, opens Lite's case and removes a pistol, admires it.

LITE
Put that damn gun down!

Lite cranks the handle and the engine roars. The Camaro reverses out and screams away.

LITE
You look like you been in a few scrapes. I mean, you're weak-lookin', but you're kinda WIRY. I bet you can handle yourself okay. Know what I mean?
If I get into hassling, man, I'm serious. Someone fucks with me, straight off, I nut 'em in the face. I'm a fighter and a winner. Know what I mean?
I walk into someone's place of work, they're shitscared. They know I ain't no cop. They think I've come to kill 'em. And I would. I'd kill anyone that crosses me. Know what I mean?

Otto roots in the glove compartment, under the seats. Lite pulls out a tape, puts it in the cassette player.

LITE
Like music? Then you gotta LOVE this. I was into these dudes before anybody. Party with 'em all the time. Asked me to be their manager. Called bullshit on that. Managing a pop group's no job for a MAN. Know what I mean?

Otto shows Lite a gaily wrapped birthday present. Lite throws it out the window. The present explodes in the road. It is full of money. Other presents follow suit.

LITE

You read that book I gave you?

OTTO

What book?

Book I
gave you - ?,

LITE

Dioretix. Science of Matter Over Mind.

Reading that
Books

OTTO

I think I left it at the Yard.

talks to god...

LITE

You better read it, kid. And quick. That book will change your life. I found it in a Maserati in Beverly Hills. Know what I mean?

RAILROAD SWITCHING YARD. EXTERIOR. DAY

Otto tosses Lite's book into Miller's drum. Miller drops a white wedding dress on top of it. He sets them on fire and rubs his hands.

MILLER

A lot of people don't realize what's really going on. They view life as a bunch of unconnected incidents and things. They don't realize that there's this like . . . lattice of coincidence that lays on top of everything. I'll give you an example. Show you what I mean. Suppose you're thinking about a plate of shrimp. Suddenly somebody'll say like, "plate," or "shrimp," or "plate of shrimp" — out of the blue. No explanation. No point in looking for one either. It's all part of a cosmic unconsciousness.

OTTO

You eat a lot of acid, Miller? Back in Hippie days?

MILLER
I'll give you another instance. You know the way
everybody's into weirdness right now? Books in all the
supermarkets about Bermuda Triangles? UFOs? How
the Mayans invented television? That kind of thing.

OTTO
I don't read them books.

MILLER
Well, the way I see it, it's exactly the same. There ain't
no difference between a flying saucer and a time
machine. People get so hung up on specifics, they miss
out on seein' the whole thing. Take South America for
example. In South America, thousands of people go
missing every year. Nobody knows where they go. They
just like disappear. But if you think about it for a
minute, you realize something. There had to be a time
when there was no people, right?

OTTO
Yeah, I guess.

MILLER
Well where did all these people come from? Hmm? I'll
tell you where. The Future. Where did all these people
disappear to? Hm?

OTTO
The past.

MILLER
That's right. And how'd they get there?

OTTO
How the fuck do I know?

MILLER
Flying saucers, which are really . . . yeah, you got it . . .
time machines. I think a lot about this kind of stuff. I

do my best thinkin' on the bus. That's how come I don't
drive, see.

OTTO
You don't even know how to drive.

MILLER
I don't want to know how. I don't want to learn. See,
the more you drive, the less intelligent you are.

Otto shrugs and walks away.

A tear trickles down Miller's grimy cheek. He douses the fire with gasoline.

IMPALA. EXTERIOR. NIGHT

*Otto and Bud within. Otto drives. Bud coughs consumptively and smokes
Commanders. Oil refineries in the windshield.*

RADIO VOICE
— the mellowest of the mellow sounds KROQ continues
with another Nelson Riddle Medley played by
Mantovani's Strings—

Otto's hand steals toward the dial.

BUD
When a MAN takes up COMMANDER he sets all other
smokes aside.
(eyes the radio)
Leave it alone.

Otto gazes out the window. Big plane passes overhead.

OTTO
You ever wish one of those big planes would explode?
One of those big jet planes?

BUD
Nope.

65

OTTO
Me either. Never wished one of those GREAT BIG 747's
would just CRACK UP! EXPLODE! BURST INTO
FLAMES! RIGHT NOW!

BUD
You know, I think I saw one of those things once. Them
UFOs. Anyway, it was really, it was kind of scary. It
had all these colored lights and uh, sounds, I mean
sounds and lights like nothing you ever heard of before.
I mean it was really weird . . .

OTTO
Bud . . .

BUD
Yeah?

OTTO
Do you think all repo men follow the code?

BUD
Of course. Now, I mean you see a lot of fucked-up cars
come in, but ninety-nine times out of a hundred, it's the
customer who fucks them up. Assholes.

TELEPHONE BOOTH. EXTERIOR. NIGHT

Bud talks into the telephone.

BUD
Lagarto Rodriguez. Spread the word. I'm offering a
thousand dollars for his Falcon. Know what that is? It's
a BRIBE. A GRAND to show me where his car is at.
Hello? . . . Prick.

RODRIGUEZ APARTMENT. INTERIOR. NIGHT

Suave interior. NAPO *talking on the phone. Suspicious-looking crates.*

66

NAPO
What the hell is this? Who the fuck are you calling?

A LITTLE GIRL *hands* LAGARTO *one of the boxes Lite and Otto threw out of the car. Lagarto opens it. It is full of cash.*

LAGARTO
Gracias, Nina . . .

Napo sits at a table with a half-assembled machine gun. Marlene watches as he reads a printout. She wears urban outlaw gear. The little girl starts making paper airplanes. They fly past the characters for the rest of the scene.

MARLENE
Well?

NAPO
We never ripped this car.

MARLENE
I know. I asked if you can find it.

NAPO
We don't FIND cars, Marlene. We make 'em
DISAPPEAR.

MARLENE
This one is different. This one's worth twenty grand.

NAPO
TWE—you can buy ten of 'em for that!

MARLENE
Think you can find it now?

NAPO
Sesente-siete Chevy Malibu, platas Nuevo Mexico. Que dices, Lagarto?

LAGARTO
No problema.

MARLENE
Good. Let's go.

NAPO
Not so fast, Marlene. How come this junker's worth so
much? What's in it—drugs?

LAGARTO
Hermanos Rodriguez don't approve of drugs.

MARLENE
Neither do I, but it's my birthday. (*looking out window at
Bud*) That motherfucker's still down there.

*Unnoticed, the little girl makes the printout into a paper airplane. She
chucks it. It sails out the window . . .*

RODRIGUEZ APARTMENT. EXTERIOR. NIGHT

*Bud stands outside the pad. Moonrise. He shakes a fist at glowing pent-
house windows.*

BUD
Repo Man don't care how long it takes, assholes! Repo
Man's got ALL NIGHT EVERY NIGHT!

*Something lands at his feet. A paper airplane. He picks it up, unfolds
the printout. Reads.*

BUD
Jesus Christ. Twenty thousand dollars.

VIDEO VAN. INTERIOR. DAY

*Female hands encased in gloves toy with a Happy Face button. Ringing
tone. Tape cassette runs. Willowy harp music.*

68

LEILA (V.O.)
Hi, this is Leila. I'm not here right now, so please leave
your name, number and a brief message, and the time
you called at the beep. Please try to be frank.

OTTO (V.O.)
Hey, Leila, all right. This is Otto. The guy that gave
you the ride and stuff. I heard something about THAT
car.

LEILA (V.O.)
Otto . . .

*Agent Rogersz chews on the Happy Face badge. She listens as her
machines record.*

UFO HEADQUARTERS. EXTERIOR. DAY

Otto parks outside. He climbs the steps and rings the bell. A THIRD
BLOND MAN *in an unmarked car takes Otto's photograph. The door opens.
Otto slips inside.*

UFO HEADQUARTERS. INTERIOR. DAY

*Interconnecting offices with venetian blinds. Maps on the walls depict
UFO trajectories, flight paths. Clippings, fliers, photographs, Happy
Face insignia everywhere.*

The UFO CULTISTS *are all white, middle class, and beaming. They range
in age from eighteen to eighty-eight. A blissed-out* LADY *buttonholes Otto
in the doorway.*

LADY
We Happy-Facers come from every walk of life, from
governors to garbagemen. We chose the HAPPY FACE
as our symbol because it is happy but also because it is
saucer-shaped, and round, an emblem of the HAPPY
FUTURE that awaits us following the MASSIVE
CONTACTS due to occur real soon.

Leila comes out of an office holding project bluebook documents.

The beaming lady waits expectantly. Otto whispers:

> OTTO
> We must speak alone.

> LEILA
> Come this way.

They pass thru the office, weaving around SMILING ENTHUSIASTS. *Leila leads Otto into the*

VAULT. INTERIOR. DAY

She shuts the door. Otto jumps her and proceeds to make out ferociously. With difficulty, Leila pushes him away.

> LEILA
> OTTO . . . Otto, stop. You said you had something to tell me. Otto, Otto . . .

> OTTO
> Huh?

> LEILA
> What did you want to tell me?

> OTTO
> Oh. Take off your clothes.

> LEILA
> I'm at WORK, Otto.

> OTTO
> Oh yeah, me too.

> LEILA
> Your work's different than mine.

OTTO
(*dropping his pants*)
Says who?

LEILA
What're you doing? Don't do that.

OTTO
The least you could do is give me a blow job.

Leila slaps Otto.

OTTO
I guess that means no.

Another UFO enthusiast, DEIRDRE, enters the room.

DEIRDRE
LEILA . . . we have a cell meeting in two minutes time.

LEILA
Thanks, Deirdre. I'll be right there.

She slaps Otto again and leaves.

MULLHOLLAND DRIVE. EXTERIOR. NIGHT

Impala and Camaro parked overlooking the glittering valley. Piece of folded paper passes between cars. Sniffing sounds.

BUD'S VOICE
That motherfucker Oly. Thinks I don't know what's going on. Soon as I find that Chevy I'm going INDY. Gonna buy myself a tow truck, couple pit bulls, rent a yard. Gonna sit behind a desk and watch the punks do all the work . . .

LITE'S VOICE
No way you'll do that on twenty grand.

BUD'S VOICE
Oh yes you can. Long as your credit record's clean. And
mine is SPOTLESS.

LITE'S VOICE
Man, if I find that Malibu you won't see me for dust.
I'm gonna move to Mendocino County, raise myself a
bumper crop of BRUSSELS SPROUTS . . . Know what
I mean?

IMPALA. INTERIOR. DAY

Bud tosses back a drink. Otto is nodding out beside him.

BUD
Credit is a sacred trust . . . it's what our free society is
founded on. Do you think they give a damn about their
bills in Russia? I said do you think they give a damn
about their bills in Russia!!

OTTO
They don't pay bills in Russia. It's all free.

BUD
All free. Free my ass! What are you a fuckin' commie?
Huh?

OTTO
I ain't no commie.

BUD
You better not be. I don't want no commies in my car!
No Christians either!

CAR WASH. EXTERIOR. NIGHT

Kevin is lecturing his CO-WORKERS. *J. Frank drives up.*

KEVIN
I told you, no sluffing off or petting on the job. Mr.
Pace is going to be very angry. You ARE going to vote
Harry Pace for City Controller aren't you? I used to
babysit his kids. He's a fair man, but he isn't gonna
be fair when he finds out about this. You wait right
here, I'll deal with you later. I have a customer to
attend to.

GUY
Fuck you!

Kevin goes to wait on J. Frank

KEVIN
Hi, I'm Kevin. Vacuum, sir?

J. FRANK
Have you any machines?

KEVIN
What kind of machines?

J. FRANK
Machines. With food in them.

KEVIN
You don't want to eat from a machine. Go across the
street. Del Taco. They got great encharitos.

J. FRANK
But I DO want to eat from a machine. Vended food
contains all the nutrients necessary for survival.
TASTES DAMN GOOD TOO, BY GOLLY!

KEVIN
Hmmm.

73

J. FRANK
And plus, on any given evening the machine which last night gave me Cheetos might instead dispense Doritos, Oreos, YoHos, Tostidos, or Lorna Doones. You see?

KEVIN
Lorna Doones? I love Lorna Doones. All we got left is Ding Dongs.

J. FRANK
The randomness of it all is quite apalling. It is, in fact, too random to be random.

Kevin points him to the junk machine. J. Frank walks off and vomits.

KEVIN
Want me to get the trunk?

J. Frank does not appear to hear. Kevin approaches the trunk. Suddenly a Falcon convertible swings into the forecourt.

KEVIN
Hi, I'm Kevin.

NAPO
Hey, buddy, how you doin', huh? Hey, don't you remember me? I was here yesterday. Huh. Listen, I think I left a book of matches over in your office over there. You wanna go check for me?

KEVIN
Sure thing!

NAPO
Hey, thanks a lot, buddy.

KEVIN
Hey, anything for you babes.

NAPO
All right, you're beautiful, I love you.

KEVIN
Be right back.

Kevin sprints to the office. Lagarto gets out of the Falcon and enters the Malibu. The keys are in the lock. He starts it up. The Falcon and the Malibu make tracks.

STREET. EXTERIOR. NIGHT

Motorcycles tear down street, weaving across lanes.

MRS. PARKS'S HOUSE. INTERIOR. NIGHT

Otto sits on the sofa beside MRS. DEMETRIUS PARKS, *a large black woman in a robe and curlers. They drink tea. Magazines in neat rows on the table. The TV is on. Central American war news. Happy Face cushions.*

OTTO
It's really very simple, Mrs. Parks. You don't want me
to take your car, and I don't want to take your car. Now
I said to the boss, I said, look, I do not want to
repossess this lady's car.

MRS. PARKS
Well, I've been in the hospital, you see.

OTTO
Yeah. Yes, yes, I understand. My job is really on the
line over this one. I mean I could lose it right away.

MRS. PARKS
I'll see if I can borrow some money from somewhere.

OTTO
That's terrific. Really terrific.

Several very large black mod BIKERS *come into the house. One of them is* GARY PARKS, *carrying a guitar. They eye Otto icily.*

> MRS. PARKS
> Oh, how was the rehearsal, son?

> GARY
> Okay. Who's this?

> MRS. PARKS
> Oh, this is Mr. Otto, Gary, from the finance company.
> He's been telling me that he isn't going to take the car
> this time, even though he could.

Otto struggles to close his briefcase, drink his tea, and leave.

> OTTO
> Well, ah . . . better be going here . . .

> MRS. PARKS
> Do you like the tea?

> OTTO
> The tea. Yeah, it was terrific. Thank you.

> MRS. PARKS
> You're welcome.

MRS. PARKS'S HOUSE. EXTERIOR. NIGHT

*Otto emerges carrying his briefcase. Mrs. Parks's Olds is right outside.
Otto looks up and down the street. No one in sight. He pulls out keys
and hops into the car.*

> MRS. PARKS (V.O.)
> I gave you the money to pay it last week, and you didn't
> do it. What did you do with it? I'm so tired of giving
> you money . . .

OLDS. INTERIOR. NIGHT

Otto locks the doors. He puts his key in the ignition. The car starts easily. He puts his foot down. The car doesn't move.

> MRS. PARKS (V.O.)
> . . . I know what ya done. Y'all went out dancin' somewhere, that's what you did with it. Now listen, the next time I give you some money, I want you to put it on the car, y'hear. Ya working. How come you didn't do it? You're gonna be sorry, honey. Now, you boys . . .

MRS. PARKS'S HOUSE. EXTERIOR. NIGHT

The back wheels spin ferociously. The rear end of the car is jacked up off the ground.

OLDS. INTERIOR. NIGHT

Otto jams the gas pedal feverishly. The mods emerge from Mrs. Parks's and advance on the car. They pull Otto out and beat him with their guitars.

REPO OFFICE. INTERIOR. NIGHT

Miller bandages Otto's head. Otto is messed up. Plettschner lurks triumphantly.

> PLETTSCHNER
> Some people ain't cut out to be a Repo Man. Why don't you smarten up, kid?

> OTTO
> Fuck you, Plettschner. Owww. Owww.

> PLETTSCHNER
> Don't you say "fuck you" to me. Don't you know who I am?

OTTO
Yeah, you're Plettschner.

PLETTSCHNER
You're fuckin' right, I'm Plettschner. Arnold
Plettschner. Three times decorated in two world wars. I
was killing people when you were still swimming around
in your father's balls. You little scumbag. I worked five
years in a slaughter house and ten years as a prison
guard in Attica.

OTTO
So what?

PLETTSCHNER
SO WHAT? So never say "fuck you" to me. 'Cause you
haven't earned the right yet.

The door opens. Bud enters and sees Otto and laughs.

OTTO
What's so fucking funny? I almost got killed.

BUD
Aww . . .

Bud opens the refrigerator, pops a drink. He knocks it back and starts
another one. Heads toward the door.

BUD
What you got for me, Marlene?

MARLENE
Country Squire in Signal Hill. A sitting duck till dawn.

BUD
Guess I'll need a CONTRACT DRIVER . . .

Bud's eyes scan the room. Otto doesn't move.

BUD
He's THINKING. Finally. At last. And suddenly that
unemployment line's beginning to look mighty tempting,
am I right? Well go ahead. Go be a homo welfare
chiseler, just like Miller always said you were.

MILLER
I never said—

BUD
Shaddup. 'Cause frankly I don't give a damn. I never
said that it was easy, Ace. Bein' a REPO MAN's a
DAMN TOUGH MAN'S JOB ONLY A MAN CAN
DO. It ain't for pussywhips or piss-ante punks. See you
around.

Bud exits. Lite drives up.

LITE
Hey, kid. I need a contract driver.
(Otto hesitates)

PLETTSCHNER
See what I mean, punk?

Otto gets up and follows Lite.

OTTO
Fuck you.

PLETTSCHNER
Fuck you! You little scumbag!

LITE
Shut up, Plettschner.

PLETTSCHNER
Don't you ever tell me to shut up!

MALIBU. INTERIOR. NIGHT

Lagarto drives. Napo sits beside him. They cruise down a bright commercial street. They sweat profusely. Spanish war news on the radio.

> NAPO
> Que calor, eh!

> LAGARTO
> Si.

> NAPO
> It's so hot I think them drogas gonna melt. Maybe I
> better take a look.

> LAGARTO
> Don't worry about it.

> NAPO
> I can't help worrying about it. This Chevy ain't worth
> shit. Only thing that matters is the merchandise. It melts
> on us, we're liable. Pull over and I'll take a look—

MALIBU CAFE. EXTERIOR. NIGHT

Lagarto pushes Napo out of the car.

> LAGARTO
> Go buy us two sodas.

> NAPO
> What about the trunk!?

> LAGARTO
> As far as we're concerned this car don't have a trunk.
> We're just the delivery boys. VAMONOS.

Napo enters the cafe. Lagarto drums his fingers on the wheel. J. Frank's artifacts are scattered on the dashboard. Lagarto picks up a piece of paper, studies it. He gets out of the Malibu and enters the phone booth.

MARLENE
Helping Hand.

LAGARTO
Marlene. We found the car.

FIRE ESCAPE. EXTERIOR. NIGHT

A BURGLAR ALARM RINGS. *Duke and Debbi clatter down the ladder, followed by Archie. They wear black burglar clothes. Archie carries paper bags. The bags spill pills.*

DEBBI
Fuckheads! Which way's the CAR?

Duke and Archie point in different directions. She leads them running down the street. SIRENS.

DUKE
Get the lead out!

DEBBI
Quit pushing, Duke.

ARCHIE
You dropped the medications.

DUKE
It's cool dude; we got more.

DEBBI
Let me help you, Archie dear.

They run away singing, "Ride of the Valkyries."

MALIBU CAFE. EXTERIOR. NIGHT

Lagarto is in the phone booth with his back to the street. Duke, Debbi, and Archie run across the road.

LAGARTO
Yeah, well that's not the only thing Marlene; this car's
hot.

MARLENE
What do you mean, stolen?

LAGARTO
No, I mean it's hot, really hot.

MARLENE
Hot?

LAGARTO
Yeah, we're sweatin' like pigs, man.

*Duke, Debbi, and Archie canter past the car. Debbi pulls up. She runs
back and checks it out. The motor is running. Debbie jumps in and drives
after the boys. Napo emerges from the cafe with two Orange Bangs.
Lagarto steps out of the booth.* No Malibu!

OIL REFINERY STREET. EXTERIOR. NIGHT

Lite and Otto driving.

LITE
Me, fight in the war man? Fuck, no way. Nobody gotta
do that shit. Not in this country. New ID don't cost no
more than a pink slip. Know what I mean?
(*no answer*)
Something wrong?

OTTO
Nah. You know Marlene? She's pretty hot.

LITE
Otto, my man. I jumped on that action on day one.
Found out where she was coming from. (*laughs*)

They park in front of a house with a Mustang parked outside.

> OTTO
> There it is.

> LITE
> Have fun.

Otto slim jims the car. He gets in and starts hot wiring it with gum paper. A GUNSHOT. *The window smashes.*

> OTTO
> Oh shit . . . Holy shit . . . LITE . . . !

Otto throws himself on the ground. More SHOTS *ring out.*

Lite pulls up and Otto tries to get in his car.

> OTTO
> LITE! LITE! OPEN THE DOOR. THERE'S A
> MANIAC . . . WHAT ARE YOU DOING?!!

Lite gets out of the car and starts firing back at the house.

> OTTO
> OPEN THE DOOR . . . WHAT ARE YOU DOING?
> Come on, open the door!

Lite pushes him back toward the Mustang.

> LITE
> You're still on the job, white boy. Get in the car.

> OTTO
> Open the fucking door!

> LITE
> GET IN THE CAR!

OTTO
JESUS CHRIST!!

The sound of SIRENS *as both cars take off.*

DIRT LOT. EXTERIOR. NIGHT

Otto and Lite stand beside their cars. Otto is nervously drinking beer.

OTTO
You're crazy, Lite. You can't just shoot into people's
houses. Maybe you shot the guy.

LITE
What if I did?

OTTO
Well, I don't know. I mean that's pretty severe.

Lite shoots at Otto's feet.

OTTO
Jesus Christ!

LITE
Hey, blanks get the job done too.

OTTO
You repo men, man . . . you guys are all out to fuckin'
lunch. Let's get out of here.

PHONE BOOTH. EXTERIOR. DAY

Sound of DISTANT GUNSHOTS. *Leila waits beside the phone. She wears
a Happy Face badge. The phone rings. She grabs it.*

LEILA
Hello?

Lite is Sy Richardson.
"Blanks get the job done too."

      J. FRANK'S VOICE
Epi;f upi ½trgrt yp d;ofr fpem pt ftpem om tsxpt n;
sfrd?

      LEILA
I can't hear you. Is it you?

      J. FRANK'S VOICE
Pg vpitd oy'd ,r. Ejp r;dr epi;f?

      LEILA
This is Leila. Are you using a scrambler?

PHONE BOOTH ACROSS THE STREET. EXTERIOR. DAY

*J. Frank leans heavily against the door. A Matador turns the corner and
approaches, fast.*

Mad scientist J. Frank Parnell is played by Fox Harris.

J. FRANK
I can't hear you. I'm using a scrambler.

LEILA'S VOICE
:ppl piy! ;ppl piy!

J. FRANK
What?

The Matador hurtles toward him. J. Frank unscrews his scrambling device.

LEILA'S VOICE
LOOK OUT!!

J. Frank looks up and sees the Matador almost upon him. He dives out of the booth. SMASH!! *The Matador eradicates the phone booth and severs a fire hydrant. Water shower.*

MATADOR. INTERIOR. DAY

Air bags inflate in front of the blond men, pinning them to their seats.

STREET. EXTERIOR. DAY

J. Frank gets up and runs away. Leila arrives upon the scene of pandemonium. The blond men stagger out enveloped by their bags. The Chevy Malibu cruises thru the rain . . .

STREET. EXTERIOR. DAY

Leila is walking down the street when a car pulls up, AGENT E, *a blond agent, leaps from his Matador and drags her into it.*

AGENT E
Happy face. Do you want a ride?

LEILA
NO! Help, help! No! No!

VAN. INTERIOR. DAY/NIGHT

THREE MEN *and Agent Rogersz are monitoring:*

> LEILA'S VOICE
> What do you want from me?

> AGENT E'S VOICE
> We ask the questions.

> LEILA'S VOICE
> You're not going to torture me, are you?

> AGENT E'S VOICE
> Torture you? What for?

> LEILA'S VOICE
> To find out what I know. I'd torture someone in a
> second, if it was up to me.

> AGENT E'S VOICE
> Huh. Why are you looking for the Malibu?

> LEILA'S VOICE
> Because of the trunk. The aliens inside.

> AGENT E'S VOICE
> Illegal aliens?

> LEILA'S VOICE
> No, silly. Extraterrestrials.

> AGENT E'S VOICE
> Oh. (*laughs*) Did you ever think about joining the
> C.I.A.?

> LEILA'S VOICE
> I . . . . . . my boyfriend.

AGENT E'S VOICE
Boyfriend?

REPO YARD. EXTERIOR. DAY

*Otto gets out of his car. He senses something is wrong. The repo men are
gathered waiting for him. They pass a bottle of generic Jack Daniels
around and sing "Jingle Bells." Oly is cutting Miller's hair.*

OLY
Who done it to you, son?

OTTO
Who done what?

BUD
Who done WHAT, he says! Talk about GUTS! Your
FACE.

OTTO
Some dude. It doesn't matter.

LITE
Yes it does.

MARLENE
Why don't you do something, Plettschner? Aren't you a
cop or something?

PLETTSCHNER
I'm on my coffee break.

BUD
REPO MAN don't go crying to the MAN, Marlene!
REPO MAN GOES IT ALONE!

REPO MEN
Damn straight he does! Yes siree bob! Let's GO!

Plettschner (Richard Foronjy), Miller (Tracey Walter),
and Oly (Tom Finnegan)

They take huge gulps from the liter of generic J.D.

MARLENE
Just like John Wayne.

OLY
Damn right like JOHN WAYNE! What's wrong with
that?

PLETTSCHNER
Greatest American that ever lived!

MILLER
John Wayne was a fag.

REPO MEN
(*in aghast unison*)
THE HELL HE WAS!

MILLER
He was too, you boys. I installed two-way mirrors in his
pad in Brentwood. He came to the door in a DRESS.

OLY
That doesn't mean he was a homo, Miller. A lot of
regular guys like to watch their buddies fuck. I know I
do. Don't you?

LITE
FUCK JOHN WAYNE! Tell us his name you little
prick!

OTTO
Fuck you!

*Otto turns to walk away. Lite and Oly pounce on Otto, pin his arms
and lift him up into the air.*

OLY
You're taking this too personal, son. Thing is, a Repo
Man got beat up in the line of duty. It doesn't matter
that it's you. The only thing that matters is, the dude
that done it has to pay the price. Now stop being selfish
and tell us his name.

*Otto remains silent. Lite twists his arms. Oly sighs and stubs his cigar
out on Otto's neck —*

OTTO
AAAAAAAAARRRRRGGGGHHH! All right! His name
is —

91

FREEWAY. EXTERIOR. NIGHT

The repo men drive south in the Impala. They all wear distinctive baseball caps and mirror shades.

SUBURBAN DOORSTEP. EXTERIOR. NIGHT

Lite, Bud, and Miller lurk in the bushes. They wield baseball bats. Oly knocks on the door. It opens. Mr. Assistant Manager Humphries appears.

>   OLY
> Mr. Humphries?

>   MR. HUMPHRIES
> Yes . . .

Oly's bat lands square on his head. The other bats all follow suit. Kevin is seen lurking in the background by the Christmas tree.

CUT TO—
Kevin being dragged along behind the Impala.

REPO OFFICE. INTERIOR. NIGHT

Marlene types. Plettschner does his knitting. Otto sits with his feet on Oly's desk reading Outlaws of Democracy, *a repo/girly magazine. The radio plays.*

>   RADIO VOICE
> —Secretary of Defense Rudebager denied that Allied
> forces have used nerve gas against Nicaragua. He went
> on to attack the press—

The PHONE RINGS. Marlene picks it up.

>   MARLENE
> Helping Hand Acceptance Corporation. Marlene
> speaking.
> *(to Otto)*
> It's for you. A girl.

Otto.
"Keep makin' me money, kid."

LEILA'S VOICE
Hi, Otto. It's Leila.

OTTO
Leila who?

NIGHTCLUB. INTERIOR. NIGHT

Leila and Agent Rogersz share a table. Otto sits opposite them. The
CIRCLE JERKS, *clad in matching red, yellow, blue, and green tuxedos,*
play their popular hit, "When the Shit Hits the Fan."

AGENT ROGERSZ
You may be wondering why I have summoned you here
tonight.

OTTO
(*to Leila*)
Who's your weird friend?

LEILA
Otto, this is Agent Rogersz. She works for the
Government.

OTTO
Uh huh? I thought the Government was, like, ah, on the
other side . . .

LEILA
I thought so too. But, Otto, I was wrong. Agent Rogersz
wants to help us find the aliens. There isn't much time . . .

Otto nods skeptically. He stares at the band.

OTTO
I used to LIKE these guys.

Agent Rogersz raps the table with her metal hand.

AGENT ROGERSZ
I work for a Special Agency. This Agency is so secret it
has no name. Its purpose is to prepare the free world for
the arrival of EXTRATERRESTRIAL
INTELLIGENCES. The means we use are the mass
media. Movies, video games, TV, the press. Do you
follow me?

LEILA
Agent Rogersz thinks J. Frank is in trouble, Otto. She
thinks that's why he hasn't made contact. She thinks
there's SOMEONE ELSE involved.

94

Both look at Otto expectantly. Otto finishes his drink.

AGENT ROGERSZ
CERTAIN PEOPLE would pay a lot of ROUBLES for
our aliens, Otto. These E.T.s are a National Treasure.
For the sake of this and future generations you MUST
tell us everything you know.
(drums her metal fingers)
Well?

OTTO
I'm thinking. Can I have another drink?

LEILA
Otto! These aliens aren't on ICE or ANYTHING! They
could be starting to DECAY. We have to find them
before they turn into MUSH.

DUKE'S VOICE
WELL! If it ain't the REPO MAN!

*Otto looks up in alarm. Duke, Debbi, and Archie weave toward them
—out of their heads. They wear designer punk attire.*

ARCHIE
You look like SHIT you WANKER! AHAHAHA!

OTTO
Duke. Debbi. Archie. These are Leila and her Weird
Friend. Leila, these are—

*Debbi spits in Leila's drink. Duke grabs Otto's lapels and starts to drag
him 'round the room.*

DUKE
Howya fuckin' doin', buddy?

ARCHIE
How come you don't hang out with your friends no more?

95

OTTO
What friends?

DUKE
Want some BYOOT, DUDE?

Duke sticks a vial of butyl nitrate under Otto's nose. His fingers fumble and he drops the bottle on the table.

DEBBI/ARCHIE
DUKE!

Debbi and Archie fall to the table and snort evaporating engine anti-knock fluid. Agent Rogersz looks at Leila in disgust. Duke hangs onto Otto's shirt.

DUKE
I really love ya, man. You're my best friend. Cause you always fuckin' came to see me while I was in Juvy.

OTTO
I was busy, man. I told you, I was workin'.

Debbie sees Agent Rogersz's metal hand.

DEBBI
Ooh . . . look, a metal hand.

ARCHIE
Cool. *(laughs)*

DEBBI
Can we feel it?

Archie kisses the hand.

Debbi kisses the hand too, more intensely.

DUKE
Fuck this. Let's go do some crimes.

Debbi sticks her hands down Duke's pants. Duke smirks. Duke, Debbi, and Archie leave, tipping the doorman handsomely.

> LEILA
> Charming friends you have there, Otto.

> OTTO
> Thanks. I made 'em myself.

PARKING LOT. EXTERIOR. NIGHT

The three punks stagger 'round the corner. In the lot sits the Chevy Malibu, minus license plates. J. Frank is trying to pick the lock with a coat hanger.

> J. FRANK
> Poor baby. Hasn't had a wash in days.

> DEBBI
> HEY! What are you doing with our car?

J. Frank straightens slowly. He seems sicker than before.

> J. FRANK
> YOUR car?

The punks surround him. Duke feints. No response.

> ARCHIE
> Yeah. Fuck off.

> J. FRANK
> Are you sure? It looks like mine. Does it have pecan pies in the back seat?

> ARCHIE
> Not any more. We ate 'em!

> DUKE
> Shut up, Archie.

97

ARCHIE
You shut up.

DUKE
(to J. Frank)
You still here?

J. FRANK
My car looks just like this. But this is yours. Your car.
Of course.
(suddenly)
What's in the trunk?

DUKE
What do you mean?

J. FRANK
If this is your car then you know what's in it. Everybody
knows what's in their trunk. DON'T YOU?

DEBBI
Kickim in the nuts, Duke!

DUKE
Course I do. Giddadahere. WHAT'S SO FUCKING
FUNNY!!

J. FRANK
You are. You don't know what's in your own trunk.
And you know what? I think you're afraid to find out.

DUKE
(softly)
I ain't afraid of nothing. See.

J. FRANK
I don't blame you for being afraid.

DUKE
I SAID I AIN'T AFRAID OF NOTHING! I KILL
PEOPLE LIKE YOU!!

J. FRANK
Oh well. I guess you're right. It's better not to look.

Duke marches to the rear of the car. J. Frank backs off.

J. FRANK
Beautiful evening. You can almost see the stars.

Infuriated, Duke seizes the handle. It burns his hand.

DUKE
OWWW! This thing is HOT!

Duke pulls his bandanna off, wraps it around his hand. He grabs the handle again, starts lifting the lid.

Brilliant light floods out. There is a HISSING SOUND.

DEBBI
CLOSE IT! DUKE! NO!!

Mesmerized, Duke continues lifting. Debbi throws herself against him, knocks him down. The trunk slams shut.

ARCHIE
Ohhh . . . Dukie-Wookie hurt his widdle hand.

DUKE
Fuck you, Archie. Just for that you're not in the gang
anymore.

ARCHIE
I'm taking over now. King Archie! The Invincible!

> DEBBI
> Shut up, Archie.

> ARCHIE
> Hey, Debbie, watch this.

Archie opens the trunk. He is VAPORIZED.

> J. FRANK
> Oh dear, what a shame.

> DEBBI
> Come on, Duke, let's go do those crimes.

> DUKE
> Yeah, yeah, let's go get sushi and not pay.

FALCON. INTERIOR. NIGHT

Rodriguez Brothers cruise the nighttime streets. Napo pores over Thomas Bros. Lagarto drives.

> NAPO
> Malibu, Malibu. Ever been to Malibu, Lagarto?

> LAGARTO
> Why would I go there?

CB RADIO CRACKLES. Marlene's voice:

> MARLENE (V.O.)
> ScanCar and Associated Circuits, breaker breaker. Hot leads on the Malibu in San Pedro, Thousand Oaks, and Pasadena. All operatives respond—

> NAPO
> Know what I feel like? A fuckin' REPO MAN. How about Pasadena—
> *(the Malibu passes the other way)*
> MIRA! LA BAMBA!

Lagarto slams into a hard U-turn.

2ND STREET TUNNEL. EXTERIOR. NIGHT

J. Frank rolls along, unaware of the Rodriguez Brothers close behind. His car is suffused with a greenish light.

> REV. LARRY (V.O.)
> Now there's a very special date I'd like y'all to write down on your calendar. The 5th of April 1999 —

J. Frank reaches for his pocket diary.

3RD AND FLOWER. EXTERIOR. NIGHT.

J. Frank enters the freeway on-ramp. Lagarto does the same.

FREEWAY. EXTERIOR. NIGHT

The Falcon flashes headlights, pulls alongside the Malibu. Napo leans out, waving a wallet with a sheriff's badge.

> NAPO
> Special Deputies! Pull over!

MALIBU. INTERIOR. NIGHT

J. Frank sweats profusely. He tries to write and drive at the same time. He doesn't notice Napo.

> REV. LARRY (V.O)
> Now that might seem a ways away, but that's the date the Holy Ghost has personally told me —

IMPALA. INTERIOR. NIGHT

Bud drives the others home. Oly sits beside him telling an interminable joke. Miller and Lite consume the usual in back.

OLY

—and so the Salesman says, "How come that pig's got a wooden leg?"

BUD

How come people never CARPOOL. It's disgusting.

MILLER

If people carpooled, we'd be out of a job.

ALL

BULLSHIT!

Lite notices the Falcon. He nudges Miller.

LITE

Good lookin' car.

Miller agrees. He taps Bud on the shoulder. Bud looks across and makes eye contact with Lagarto. Lagarto flips him off.

LITE

Hey, Budski, there's your girlfriend.

BUD

Oh, those Rodriguez Brothers, huh. Okay boys, we got the whole team here tonight. Let's settle these motherfuckers' hash for good.

LITE

Let's do it.

FREEWAY. EXTERIOR. NIGHT

Bud sideswipes the Falcon.

FALCON. INTERIOR. NIGHT

Lagarto swerves right, Napo almost falls out. Lagarto drags him back.

102

He takes his foot off the gas and ducks back behind J. Frank's Malibu.

FREEWAY. EXTERIOR. NIGHT

The Impala ducks behind the Falcon. Bud stays inches from their tail, honking.

FALCON. INTERIOR. NIGHT

Lagarto slides right once again. They're in the exit lane. J. Frank is right beside them as they hurtle toward the lane divider.

NAPO
Don't lose him!

But they do.

IMPALA. INTERIOR. NIGHT

Bud flies after the Falcon in a deadly curve. Miller sees the Malibu cruising blithely away.

MILLER
You guys—

OLY
Don't interrupt me, Miller. So, anyway, the Farmer says—

BENEATH THE FREEWAY. EXTERIOR. NIGHT

Bud races alongside the Falcon. Smoke pours from the Falcon's hood. He boxes it against the concrete wall. Napo leaps snarling onto Bud's hood. Bud jumps out with his baseball bat.

LAGARTO
Too bad, Bud! This is going to cost you plenty.

BUD
What do you mean, cost ME plenty?

LAGARTO
How's your neck, Napoleon?

NAPO
Oh, my neck. Yeah . . . oh, shit . . . oh shit my neck is
killing me, man, I think I got whiplash.

LAGARTO
Besides the whiplash, this isn't a repo car.

BUD
Bullshit. I got the fucking papers.

LAGARTO
OLD! We paid it off. You see, uh, this is our favorite
car.

NAPO
That's right. You got insurance, motherfucker?

*Bud swings his bat. The other repo men grab him and try to wrestle it
away. All fall down in a struggling bundle.*

REPO OFFICE. INTERIOR. DAY

*Bud stares at an official-looking document. Oly drinks beer and watches
him. Marlene types noisily. Big flies drone.*

BUD
Bullshit.

OLY
That's what I said when the Marshall woke me up at
four this morning. Unfortunately it isn't bullshit. It's a
summons.

BUD
Bullshit. You should have refused to accept it.

OLY
HAVE YOU READ IT? We're being SUED by the
Rodriguez Brothers. For harrassment, medical expenses,
and malicious damage to a car THEY FUCKING OWN.

BUD
You know the Rodriguez Brothers, Oly. They're a pair
of scumbags.

OLY
So what. We've got to sit down and get our story
straight.

BUD
BULLSHIT! You're taking their word against mine!

OLY
I WAS THERE, REMEMBER?! Maybe you better go
home. Take the rest of the week off.

BUD
Take the rest of—I can't take the fuckin' rest—ohhh,
yeah, I get it. Take the rest of the week off, Budski, so
YOU can get the fucking twenty thousand dollars for the
Malibu.

OLY
Make it a fucking month.

BUD
Yeah, well fuck you!

OLY
On second thought, Budski—don't bother coming back
at all.

BUD
Great. I'll come back and pick up my stuff later, when
the fucking place don't stink so bad.

Plettschner laughs.

OLY
Shut up.

IMPALA. INTERIOR. DAY

*Otto drives Bud down skid row. Mexican radio commercials. Bud eyes
the sorry-looking* BUMS *suspiciously.*

BUD
Some of these people, you wonder how much money
they owe. A lot of them are on the run, don't even use
their Social Security numbers. If there was only some
way of finding out how much they owe and making 'em
pay . . .

OTTO
Oh, for Christ's sake, Bud. They're winos. They don't
have any money. You think they'd be bums if they
did?

Bud reaches over and jams them into park. The car grinds and stalls.

BUD
You want out? DO YOU?

OTTO
No. And anyway, I'm driving.

BUD
I told you before. I don't like wise guys in my car. No
wimps, no winos, no wiseacres. Commander.

Otto hands him one. He drives on in silence.

BUD

You happy in your work, Ace? I get the feeling that we
ain't communicating like we used to. When you and me
started out I felt like I could teach you something. Share
something with you—
(jams handbrake on)
ANSWER ME!

Otto throws the door open and stalks out of the car.

SKID ROW. EXTERIOR. DAY

Otto wanders along. Bums and decrepitude abound. He sees MEN AND
WOMEN *(the Art Department and Producers of this film) herded into a
van. He passes flyers pasted to a wall. They read: HARRY PACE—
CITY CONTROLLER—HARRY PACE. Harry Pace wears a
Happy Face Badge. Otto walks on. A Chevy Malibu passes by. Otto
sees it and begins to run.*

MALIBU. INTERIOR. DAY

*J. Frank rolls along. He doesn't notice anything. His gums are bleeding.
He reaches in his mouth, pulls out a tooth.*

MOLINO AND 4TH. EXTERIOR. DAY

*J. Frank enters the 4th Street bridge. Otto pursues him. The Malibu
disappears over the rise.*

4TH STREET BRIDGE. EXTERIOR. DAY

*Otto crests the rise. J. Frank is nowhere to be seen. Otto leans against
the parapet and blows his lunch. The barf lands by the Malibu, passing
underneath. Otto hurtles down the stairs.*

CAR WASH. EXTERIOR. DAY

*The Malibu emerges from the auto dry. Steam rises from the trunk. J.
Frank cruises toward the street. Otto runs up, clutching his side, collapses*

*on the corner, sticks his thumb out. J. Frank sees the hitchhiker, stops
and lets him in.*

MALIBU. INTERIOR. DAY

*J. Frank extends a hand. Otto accepts it weakly. Crumpled banknotes
and pecan pie wrappers on the dash.*

> J. FRANK
> J. Frank Parnell.

> OTTO
> O-o-o-

> J. FRANK
> Jogger? Me too. I can always tell. Something about us.
> Healthy glow. What line of work you in?

> OTTO
> R-r-r-

> J. FRANK
> Rock 'n' roller, eh? Used to be a musician myself, in
> college days. Of course it was folk songs back then, and
> protest songs. "Michael Row the Boat Ashore," Pete
> Seeger and the Weavers, wasn't that a time! I almost
> had a tryst with Ronnie Gilbert. Expect that surprises
> you!

> OTTO
> *(trying to light a Commander)*
> Never heard of him.

> J. FRANK
> Him? Hmm. You ever feel as if your mind had started
> to erode?

> OTTO
> No.

J. FRANK
That's all right. You will. You will. You ever think that maybe you were sitting on the greatest gift that Mother Nature ever gave the world? Only the world was just not old enough to use it wisely? Ever been . . . TO UTAH?

OTTO
Uh uh. Like my badge?

J. FRANK
I go to Utah every year. A friend of mine was the designer of the MX missile racetrack basing mode. A hundred thousand miles of railroad tracks in a big loop thru Utah, Arizona, and Nevada. The BOMBS were going to hide in locomotive sheds. That way the Red Team would never know exactly where they were. I still go out to Utah, just to think about the way it might have been . . .

OTTO
Sir, I represent Helping Hand Acceptance Corporation —

J. FRANK
RADIATION! Yes indeed! You hear the most outrageous LIES about it! Half-baked goggle-box do-gooders telling everyone it's bad for you! PERNICIOUS NONSENSE! Everyone can stand a hundred chest x-rays a year. They ought to have 'em too.

OTTO
Do you believe in FLYING SAUCERS?

Otto waggles his badge. J. Frank shrugs.

J. FRANK
When they cancelled the project, it almost did me in. One day my head was literally BURSTING. Next day,

109

nothing. Swept away. But I'll show them.
(*blinking*)
I had a lobotomy in the end.

OTTO
Lobotomy? Isn't that for loonies?

J. FRANK
Not at all. A friend of mine had one. Designer of the
Neutron Bomb. You know about the Neutron Bomb?
Destroys people but leaves buildings standing. Fits in a
suitcase, nobody knows it's there till BLAMMO! Eyes
melt and skin explodes and EVERYBODY DEAD. It's
so immoral working on the thing can drive you mad.
And that's what happened to this friend of mine. So he
had a lobotomy. Now he's well again.

OTTO
What kind of car does your friend drive?

J. FRANK
A Chevy Malibu.

OTTO
You do the same work? You and him?

J. FRANK
Didn't I tell you I can't tell you what I do? I'm
classified. It's classified, I mean.

OTTO
This is a neat old car. You want to let me drive?

J. FRANK
What do you mean?

OTTO
I don't know. You look kinda tired. Don't you feel . . .
funny?

J. FRANK

Why should I feel "funny"? The two hemispheres are
fundamentally at odds. Most people would be a whole
lot happier and smarter if they'd . . . that's strange . . .
I DO feel funny . . . I . . .

*J. Frank slumps forward. His head hits the dashboard hard. Otto brakes.
Gingerly he raises J. Frank's head. Blood flows from J. Frank's mouth
and nose. J. Frank is dead.*

BUS STOP. EXTERIOR. DAY

*Otto sits J. Frank's body on the bus stop bench. His head lolls to one
side. Otto tries to set it upright.* SIRENS. *Otto gets back in the Malibu
and drives away.*

REPO YARD. EXTERIOR. DUSK

*Otto locks the Malibu behind the gate. The office lights are on. The yard
is empty. A sign is taped to the gate:*

BIG PARTY AT MILLER'S CU THERE

MILLER'S HOUSE. INTERIOR. NIGHT

*Flashbulbs. It is party time. Cowboy music on the stereo. Woolworth's
art on walls. Lite, Oly, and Miller watch a football game. Their* WIVES
*eye Otto lustfully. They're all identical—fixed grins, lipstick, drunk and
extramaritally horny.*

WIFE 1

Here's the young new waver we've all heard so much
about. My old man had a mohawk when I met him. He
was in the service then. He was such a monster. I used
to have to tell him "No."

WIFE 2

My old man was exactly the same way, until we got
married.

III

LITE
Hey, Oly, your wife's hanging all over Otto.

OLY
Yeah, flies on shit.

OTTO
Have you seen Bud lately?

WIFE 3
Who?

REPO YARD. EXTERIOR. NIGHT

Gloved hand applies bolt cutters to the feeble padlock and opens the gate. The Malibu waits within.

OTTO'S PARENTS' HOUSE. INTERIOR. NIGHT

Otto lets himself in. His folks are glued to the TV. They both wear Happy Face badges.

REV. LARRY
(*on TV*)
—perhaps you know of someone that's not fighting the good fight! An idle youth who's failed to register for PATRIOTIC CHORES! If so, call this TOLL-FREE NUMBER, praise the Lord!

Wasted, lost, and miserable, Otto tries to curl up between his parents. He gets cobwebs all over him.

DAD
Haven't seen you in a while, son.

MOM
Some men were just here looking for you, Otto.

OTTO
What kind of men?

MOM
Very nice young men. They had sunglasses on.

OTTO
What did you tell them? Did you tell them I was sick?

DAD
We told them the truth, son. Gave 'em your address at
work.

Otto crumples. He crawls off the couch.

REV. LARRY
—for there is no redemption for the UNREDEEMED!
No escape for the FAIR WEATHER PATRIOTS! No
salvation from the BOILING BLISTERING FIRES
OF—

OTTO'S PARENTS' HOUSE. EXTERIOR. NIGHT

Otto douses the parents' house with gasoline. He sets it on fire.

STREET. EXTERIOR. NIGHT

Otto wanders along. He passes an Impala parked beside the curb.

BUD'S VOICE
Hey, Ace. Wait up.

IMPALA. INTERIOR. NIGHT

Bud drives with Otto in the car.

OTTO
So you want to talk about it?

BUD
Talk about what, kid?

OTTO
Why you're so damn mad at me.

BUD
I'm not mad at you, kid. I'm not. I'm not mad at you.

OTTO
All right. Okay. Where're we going?

BUD
To the liquor store.

LIQUOR STORE. EXTERIOR. NIGHT

Duke and Debbi are sitting in a car. She snorts something from a vial. Duke looks sick. Car headlights wash over them.

DUKE
Debbi . . .

DEBBI
What . . .

DUKE
I've been thinking. Now that we've got some money and Archie's gone . . . don't you think it's time we settled down? Get a little house. I want you to have my baby.

DEBBI
Why?

DUKE
Why? I don't know . . . everybody does it, 'n it seems like the thing to do. 'N . . .
(*he whimpers*)

DEBBI
Asshole.

DUKE
(*boldly*)
Let's go do the job.

Duke sighs and snorts. His hand is swollen horribly. They don their masks and get out of the car.

LIQUOR STORE. INTERIOR. NIGHT

Duke and Debbi POV — approaching the counter.

Bud and Otto are at the register with a six-pack. The supermarket guard is shopping too. He wears a coat over his uniform and a badge that says PIC'N'PAY UNFAIR.

BUD
Why don't you get this?

Otto digs in his pockets. Looks up suddenly.

OTTO
Duke. Debbi. What are you doing here?

DUKE
What's it look like?

DEBBI
UP AGAINST THE WALL!!

Duke and Debbi pull their guns. Bud draws his automatic. The supermarket guard sees only Bud's gun. He whips out his enormous piece.

GUARD
Drop it, MOTHERFUCKER!

Everybody looks at everybody else. Tension.

Debbi shoots Bud, who crash lands among the ketchup bottles. The guard shoots Duke. Duke shoots the guard. The store owner blasts Duke with a shotgun, knocking him down. Debbi shoots the store owner, aims her gun at Otto.

> OTTO
> (*with his hands up*)
> Debbi, uh, do you, uh, think it's too late for us to get romantically involved?

> DEBBI
> I think, a little.

> OTTO
> Wait, wait, stick with me. I'll make you a repo wife.

Debbi grabs a bag of chips from the counter and throws them to Otto as she leaves.

> DEBBI
> Here.

Debbi is gone. Otto drops the chips and goes to Duke, who is dying. He cradles Duke's head in his arms.

> DUKE
> Otto . . .

> OTTO
> Yeah, man.

> DUKE
> The lights are growing dim . . . I know a life of crime led me to this sorry fate . . . and yet . . . I blame society. Society made me what I am.

> OTTO
> That's bullshit. You're a white suburban punk just like me.

DUKE
But it still hurts. *(gagging horribly)*

OTTO
You're going to be all right, man.

Duke gags some more.

OTTO
Maybe not.

Bud lies amid the shattered ketchup display. Otto moves toward him. SIRENS SOUND. *He pauses. Bud does not budge. Otto turns and runs out the door.*

BUS STOP. EXTERIOR. NIGHT

The video van is parked beside the bus stop. MEN IN SUITS *cluster around J. Frank's body. Flashbulbs pop. A blond man approaches the corpse.*

AGENT ROGERSZ
Don't touch him!

A man in suit sprays J. Frank's body with a stream of gasoline. They light the corpse on fire.

REPO YARD. EXTERIOR. NIGHT

The Impala pulls up. The gate hangs open. The Chevy Malibu is gone. Otto gets out slowly. Thru the bright office window he sees two blond men with sunglasses roughing up Marlene. Without a second thought, he runs toward the office. Somebody grabs his arm—Plettschner, the cop.

PLETTSCHNER
Better stay out of this.

OTTO
Plettschner! That's Marlene!

PLETTSCHNER
It's none of our business.

Otto steps forth. Plettschner grabs his arm.

PLETTSCHNER
Hey kid! You ever think about being a chicken man?

OTTO
A what?

PLETTSCHNER
A chicken man. It's what I would have been. If things
was different. Little baby chicks running around a day

Otto and Plettschner.
"We're going to get to the bottom of this."

old. On the farm. Going in and taking the eggs. A very
sacred thing. It's like . . . taking a woman's baby. You
ever see a farmer's wife?

Otto breaks loose. He runs up the Repo Office steps.

> PLETTSCHNER
> It's peaceful . . .

REPO OFFICE. INTERIOR. NIGHT

AGENT S, *a blond man, is threatening Marlene with a staple gun.*

> AGENT S
> Maybe the bitch wants to eat staple!

*Otto comes bursting in. Marlene breaks loose and kicks Agent S in the
stomach. Her elbow catches* AGENT B *on the nose. They fall to their knees,
groaning. She polishes them off with karate blows.*

> MARLENE
> Let's go.

> OTTO
> No way, Marlene. My car is gone and we're going to get
> to the bottom of this.

> MARLENE
> *(raising a chair over Agent S)*
> Like hell we are.

> AGENT S
> Not my face!

Plettschner charges in.

> PLETTSCHNER
> Hold it, Marlene. Freeze!

> MARLENE
Over my dead body.
(drops chair on Agent S)

> PLETTSCHNER
Then that's how it's going to have to be.

> MARLENE
Come and get me. Come on.

> PLETTSCHNER
I've been wanting to do that one for a long time, honey.

> MARLENE
Come on. Come on, come on if you think you're man
enough.

> OTTO
Hey, Plettsch . . . coffee break!

Otto throws the coffee urn at Plettschner.

> PLETTSCHNER
AAAEEEAARGH!! !!!!!!!!!

*Otto bends over a fallen blond body. Marlene opens the back door. Otto
finds a wallet, opens it. Super-secret Agency I.D. He looks around.
Marlene has gone. Perturbed, Otto steps out thru the front door.*

Instant SIRENS and a glare of lights. STRUGGLING SOUNDS.

VIDEO VAN. INTERIOR. DAY

*Otto is seen on a video screen. He is strapped to a slab. Electrodes are
attached to his nipples, temples, genitals. Leila and Agent Rogersz at the
console. Agent Rogersz speaks into the microphone.*

> AGENT ROGERSZ
Good evening, Otto. This is Agent Rogersz. I am going
to ask you a few questions. Since time is short and you

may lie, I'm going to have to torture you. But I want you to know it isn't personal.

OTTO
(on TV)
Look, uh, you don't have to torture me. I'll tell you anything.

AGENT ROGERSZ
Good. Where is the Malibu?

OTTO
I don't know. Somebody ripped it from the yard —

Agent Rogersz nods to Leila. Leila pulls a lever. Electronic interference on the TV screen.

OTTO
AAAAUUUUGGGGHHHH!!

LEILA
I don't think he knows.

AGENT ROGERSZ
Increase the voltage.

LEILA
But what if he's innocent?

AGENT ROGERSZ
No one is innocent. Proceed.

Leila pushes up the voltage regulator.

OTTO
AAAAAAUUUUUUUGHHH.

On screen a light falls across Otto. Marlene and the Rodriguez Brothers rush into frame and remove Otto's electrodes. Lagarto throws Otto over his shoulder.

121

AGENT ROGERSZ
Ah yes, look at them—high heels, hair nets, those
ridiculous trench coats. They're pathetic . . .

MAN'S VOICE
Agent Rogersz, they're getting away!

AGENT ROGERSZ
It's all part of the plan.

UNDERGROUND HALLWAY. INTERIOR

Marlene and the Brothers spirit Otto down the hall. SIRENS *and flashing
lights.*

FALCON. INTERIOR. SUNSET

Lagarto hurtles along. Napo and Marlene revive Otto with smelling salts.

OTTO
Uh . . . uh . . . uh . . . uh.

MARLENE
Otto, pull yourself together.

OTTO
Marlene. What's goin' on?

MARLENE
We're going to the hospital.

MID CITY HOSPITAL. EXTERIOR. DUSK

The Falcon slides toward the hospital.

HOSPITAL LOBBY. INTERIOR. NIGHT

*Doors fly open. Otto and Marlene enter, flanked by the Brothers Rod-
riguez. The Brothers wear raincoats and are obviously armed. As they*

go by the admissions desk, an old lady standing there recognizes Otto.

> OLD LADY
> I know you. You're the one that ran into my trash!

Otto and Marlene enter an elevator. A DOCTOR *and a* NURSE *within. The Brothers block the doors. They stop* TWO LIMPING PATIENTS *from entering.*

> LAGARTO
> Out of order. Take the stairs.

The doors close.

CORRIDOR. INTERIOR. NIGHT

Otto and Marlene emerge from the elevator. They wear the doctor and the nurse's clothes. We follow them along the hall. They check all the doors. They pass a body on a gurney. Otto lifts the sheet, sees Kevin. Otto continues to check doors. A little blue Christmas tree hangs from one door handle. Otto grabs it and turns.

HOSPITAL LOBBY. INTERIOR. NIGHT

Napo leans against the wall. A blond man enters, disguised as a blind man.

HOSPITAL ROOM. INTERIOR. NIGHT

Bud lies in bed, bandages around his head. He stares unblinking at the TV screen. Rev. Larry.

> MARLENE
> Ask him about the Malibu.

> OTTO
> How ya doin', man? Look, about the other night, I'm
> sorry I split. I know I should have stayed with you, but

. . . it's like when I was a kid, you know, I had this set
of Big Wheels—

Napo enters.

> NAPO
> Psst.

It's time to go.

STAIRWAY. INTERIOR. NIGHT

*Napo, Marlene, and Otto hurtle down the stairs. They are pursued
by two blond men with guns. One blond man fires his revolver down
the stairs. The other blond man empties his shotgun. All the bullets
miss.*

> RECORDED VOICE
> Quiet in the stairwells. Quiet in the stairwells.

HOSPITAL ROOM. INTERIOR. NIGHT

> REV. LARRY
> *(on TV)*
> A very sad unchristian thing just happened. A sweet old
> lady's car was stolen. It's a Chevy Malibu. Brothers and
> sisters, please, if you've seen this car, just call this toll-
> free number . . . praise the Lord.

PARKING STRUCTURE. INTERIOR. NIGHT

*Marlene, Napo, and Otto pile out of the stairway. They leap into the
waiting Falcon. Lagarto puts his foot down and they tear away. Instantly
the Matadors appear. They pursue the Falcon into the flourescent depths.
Unnoticed, a Chevy Malibu backs out and heads for an upper exit. It
glows. Lagarto increases the distance between them. He swings hard left
for an exit and encounters SEVERE TIRE DAMAGE spikes. His tires
expire. The Matadors arrive. Marlene and Agent Rogersz leap out aiming
enormous guns.*

LAGARTO
All right, don't shoot. All right, all right.

BLOND AGENT
Chicken shit.

They make raucous chicken clucks.

AGENT ROGERSZ
Where's the Malibu?

OTTO
Don't even ask. Because I don't know. I mean I don't
have it, Marlene doesn't have it. You and your crazy
friends don't have it, so that only leaves . . .

HOSPITAL ROOM. INTERIOR. NIGHT

*Blond men kick Bud's door down. All pile in, pointing their guns. Marlene
and the Brothers are herded in. Otto too. The curtains flutter. Bud is
long gone.*

REV. LARRY
He is RISEN! Holy Jesus' Name!

ALL
Where the fuck is he!!

OTTO
Mind if I close the window?

*Otto walks over to the window and leaps through. The blond men
rush to it. Napo bumps against a* SWAT-TYPE BLOND MAN *with
tear gas cannisters hanging from his tits. He grabs the handles and
yanks them. The blond men panic. Marlene and the brothers charge the
door.*

AGENT ROGERSZ
Stop them! Get him out of here!

Pandemonium. The tear gas cannisters explode.

PARKING STRUCTURE. INTERIOR. NIGHT

Otto runs to a Matador. He picks up a wooden piling, smashes the windshield and hotwires the car.

MATADOR. INTERIOR. NIGHT

Otto drives through the night, pulling off his hospital whites.

> CAR RADIO VOICE
> Here's another weird one. Reports are coming in on an apparent hail of ice cubes south of downtown. Scientists are at a loss to explain the freak showers of tiny ice cubes . . . Yuk yuk yuk . . .

REPO YARD. EXTERIOR. NIGHT

Otto halts in a shower of ice cubes. Bud sits in the glowing Malibu. He smokes a Commander. Otto approaches the car.

> OTTO
> Weird fucking shit eh, Bud? What's going on?

> BUD
> Shit . . . eleven years of repoing cars and what have I got . . . shit.

> OTTO
> Bud, listen to me. You're sitting in a car worth twenty thousand dollars. Look, we'll turn it in, we'll take the money, we'll split it sixty-forty, you and me.

> BUD
> Who gets the sixty, kid?

      OTTO
Well, I don't know. I figured since I found the car first
that ah . . .

Bud raises his gun.

      OTTO
That you'd get it.

Lights from a helicopter overhead pick them out.

      HELICOPTER VOICE
GET AWAY FROM THE CAR. THIS IS YOUR
ONLY WARNING.

Otto backs off. Bud stays in the car.

Ice cubes shower the glowing Malibu.

OTTO
We got problems, man.

Bud stays.

OTTO
No, no, no, no, wait. Stop fucking around, man. Only
an asshole gets killed over a car.

BUD
You calling me an asshole, punk?

OTTO
Yes. I'm calling you an asshole.

BUD
COME AND GET ME, COPPER! I'M WELL
ARMED AND I KNOW WHERE YOU LIVE!

A SNIPER *in the helicopter shoots Bud.*

OTTO
Son of a fucking bitch . . .

BUD
I'd rather die on my feet than live on my knees.

The yard becomes a mass of people and fighting: SCIENTISTS, MEN IN
FIRESUITS, *repo men, agents, etc.*

LITE
Hey Oly, catch Bud.

OLY
(*arriving, waving papers*)
I have the papers on this car. You guys want a beer?

AGENT ROGERSZ
No beer is needed here!

The White Suits struggle to subdue the Chevy Malibu.

The agents grab Oly.

Two blond agents, Agents B and E, sit on the tailgate of their truck.

AGENT E
I love this job.

AGENT B
(ignoring Agent E)
Linear and inverse spectrums merge . . . to zero.

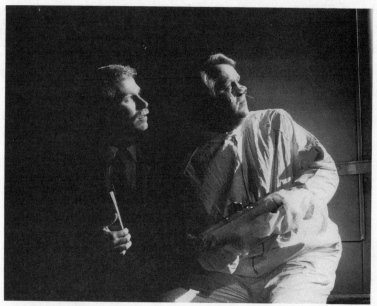

Ed Pansullo and Biff Yeager play Agent Rogersz's blond agents.

      AGENT E
It's more than a job it's a . . . a calling.

      AGENT B
Critical Mass is at a point of zero . . .

      AGENT E
You could say it's spiritual . . .

      AGENT B
Spiritual . . . ?

Reverend Larry emerges from the chopper with a Bible, holding it in front of him, staring at the luminous car. A lightning bolt zaps the Bible and lights it on fire.

REV. LARRY
Holy sheep shit!

More turmoil, shooting, wrangling. A MAN *catches on fire.*

AGENT E
Have you read this book, *Dioretix*? Chapter Seven . . .

AGENT B
I got it marked . . .

AGENT E
Verse Three.

Otto shields his eyes. He stares at the car and, thru the glare, sees Miller walking up to it, patting its sides and crooning softly. Dead silence. Miller opens the door.

OTTO
Miller! What are you doing?!!

MILLER
Goin' for a spin.

OTTO
But you don't know how to drive.

Miller smiles and gets into the car, starts it up and beckons to Otto. Otto hesitates.

LEILA
Otto, don't go. What about our relationship?

OTTO
Huh?

LEILA
Our relationship.

OTTO
(*taking off*)
Fuck that.

LEILA
You shithead. I'm glad I tortured you. How could you
leave me? I'm the one who's supposed to be in that car.

*Otto gets in the car. All aglow. Miller grins and puts the car in drive.
It starts to rise.*

OLY
Best goddamned car in the yard.

*The Malibu lifts off till it hangs thirty feet above the ground. Everyone
watches with expressions of horror/wonderment/awe as the car buzzes
downtown.*

LITE
(*to Leila*)
Need a ride, baby?

LEILA
(*brightly*)
Okay!

OTTO'S VOICE
Wow! This is INTENSE!

MILLER'S VOICE
The life of the Repo Man is always intense.

The Malibu vanishes into hyperspace.

FINIS

MAIN TITLES

MICHAEL NESMITH
PRESENTS

AN
EDGE CITY
PRODUCTION

HARRY DEAN STANTON

EMILIO ESTEVEZ

REPO MAN

OLIVIA BARASH

TRACEY WALTER

SY RICHARDSON
SUSAN BARNES

DEL ZAMORA
EDDIE VELEZ

FOX HARRIS

MICHAEL SANDOVAL
JENNIFER BALGOBIN

DICK RUDE
ZANDER SCHLOSS

Also Starring
VONETTA MCGEE

And
RICHARD FORONJY

Casting
VICTORIA THOMAS

Art Direction
J. RAE FOX
LYNDA BURBANK

Editor
DENNIS DOLAN

Music by
HUMBERTO LARRIVA
STEVEN HUFSTETER
Repo Man Theme
IGGY POP

Director of Photography
ROBBY MULLER

Executive Producer
MICHAEL NESMITH

Produced by
JONATHAN WACKS
PETER MCCARTHY

Written & Directed by
ALEX COX

END CREDITS

BUD	Harry Dean Stanton
OTTO	Emilio Estevez
MILLER	Tracey Walter
LEILA	Olivia Barash
LITE	Sy Richardson
AGENT ROGERSZ	Susan Barnes
J. FRANK PARNELL	Fox Harris
OLY	Tom Finnegan
LAGARTO	Del Zamora
NAPO	Eddie Velez
KEVIN	Zander Schloss
DEBBI	Jennifer Balgobin
DUKE	Dick Rude
ARCHIE	Michael Sandoval
MARLENE	Vonetta McGee
PLETTSCHNER	Richard Foronjy
REVEREND LARRY	Bruce White
AGENT B	Biff Yeager
AGENT E	Ed Pansullo
AGENT S	Steve Mattson
AGENT T/STUNT DOUBLE	Thomas Boyd
MR. HUMPHRIES	Charles Hopkins
MRS. PARKS	Helen Martin
MINER	Jon St. Elwood
DELILAH	Kelitta Kelly
MOTORCYCLE COP	Varnum Honey
MS. MAGRUDER	Sue Kiel
SHERIFF	David Chung

U.F.O. LADY	Cynthia Szigeti
ENGLISH DUSTBIN LADY	Dorothy Bartlett
OTTO DAD	Jonathon Hugger
OTTO MOM	Sharon Gregg
PEASON	Dale Reynolds
PAKMAN	Jac MacAnelly
ADDITIONAL BLOND AGENTS	Shep Wickham
	Gregg Taylor
	Jon Fondy
	Keith Miley
	Michael Bennett
	Brad Jamieson
	Jimmy Buffet
REPO WIFE #1	Janet Chan
REPO WIFE #2	Angelique Pettyjohn
REPO WIFE #3	Logan Carter
REPO WIFE #4	Laura Sorrenson
FIRST REPO VICTIM	George Sawaya
REPO VICTIM'S WIFE	Connie Ponce
SODA JERK/STUNT DOUBLE	Bobby Ellis
TOW TRUCK DRIVER	Quentin Gutierrez
LIQUOR STORE CLERK #1	Richard Surukawa
LIQUOR STORE CLERK #2	"Earthquake" Hesson
NIGHTCLUB BAND	The Circle Jerks:
	Keith Morris
	Greg Hetson
	Chuck Bisquits
	Earl Liberty
SCOOTER GUYS	The Untouchables:
	Clyde Grimes
	Chuck Askerneese
	Kevin Long
	Jerry Miller
	Rob Lampron
	Josh Harris
	Herman Askerneese
LAUNDRY PERSON	Kim Williams
LAUNDRY PERSON	Michele Person
DOCTOR	Wally Cronin

NURSE	Monona Wali
NURSE	Delores Deluxe
BOUNCER	Cosmo Mata
CLUB OWNER	Rodney Bengenheimer
TENNIS PLAYERS	Jorge Martinez
	Melanie Schloss
	Nancy Richardson
HARRY PACE	Con Covert
HELICOPTER PILOT	Harry Hauss
STUNTS	Eddie Hice
	Rick Barker
	Will Dawson
	Harry Wowchuk
	Rich Seaman
	Fred Scheiwiller
	Michael Walters
	Danny Kosta

Associate Producer	Gerald Olson
Production Manager	Allen Alsobrook
First Assistant Director	Betsy Magruder
Second Assistant Director	William "Rip" Murray
Set Decorator	Cheryl Cutler
Property Master	Doug Fox
Costume Designer	Theda Deramus
Wardrobe Assistant	Tim Healey
Production Sound Mixer	Steve Nelson
Boom Operator	Ian Valentine
Stunt Coordinator	Eddie Hice
Script Supervisors	Sharron Reynolds
	Brenda Weiman
First Assistant Camera	Marty Layton
Second Assistant Camera	Thomas Vanghele
Second Camera	Daniel Hainey
Second Unit Camera	Stephen Posey
Second Unit Assistant	Chris Tufty
Gaffer	Greg Gardiner
Electrician's Best Boy	Scott Guthrie

Electricians	Jim Grce
	Kevin Galbraith
Key Grip	Robert Feldman
Grip's Best Boy	Kenneth Jones
Grips	Rowdy Herrington
	Leslie Percy
	Orlando Bagwell
	Dennis Lootens
Make-Up/Hair	Sharon Frances
Assistant Make-Up/Hair	Sheri Short
	Kyle Tucy
Construction Coordinator	Doug Dick
Lead Man	John Lafia
Special Effects	Robby Knott
	Roger George
Still Photographer	Martin Turner
Production Executive	Amy Ness
Production Controller	Marsha Koff
Production Coordinator	Iya Labunka
Edge City Executive	Debbie Diaz
Creative Consultants	Dick Rude
	Brant Reiter
Thanks To	Michael Chinich
	Harry Gittes
Technical Advisor	Mark Lewis
Location Scout	Mark Anderson
Transporation Captain	David Shafer
Drivers	John Morello
	Tom Boyd
	Dan Boyd
	Bobby Ellis
	Jackie Diskin
	Hal Voelkel
	Tom Lynch
	Scott Padgent
Stunt Safety	Loren James
Craft Services	Cameron Bishop
Production Assistants	Misty Sue Carey
	Anne Van der Vort

	Steve McAfee
Police	Al Delapp
	Bill Demyen
Security	Tim Clouse
	Pat Stransky
Video Coordinator	Abbe Wool
Video Technical Director	Bruce McKrimmon
Video Camera	Tom Musca
Technical Consultant	Chuck Collett
Computer Graphics	George Seminarh
	Magda Rangel
	Steven Michael Sarno
Video Engineer	John Reeder
Supervising Sound Editor	Warren Hamilton, Jr.
Sound Editors	David Stone
	Donald Flick
Re-Recording Mixers	Michael Minkler C.A.S.
	Richard Beggs
ADR Editor	Bonnie Koehler
Supervising Asst. Editor	Janiss Garza
Assistant Editors	Steven Myers
	Joan Chapman
	Thure Gustafson
Apprentice Editors	Barbara Caporale
	Dennis Brown
Assistant Sound Editor	Christopher Flick
Foley	John Post
	Kim Fowler

ADDITIONAL PHOTOGRAPHY

Camera	Robert Richardson
Second Camera	Tom Richmond
First Assistant Camera	Michael Little
Second Assistant Camera	Chris Lombardi
Production Sound Mixer	Larry Hoki
Grip/Gaffer	Chris Centrella
Electricians	Patrick Melly
	Ramon Menendez
Property Master	Ron Seigal

Stunt Coordinator	Brad Bovee
Make-Up/Hair	Lisa Schulze
Title Design	Robert Dawson
Opticals	Movie Magic
Negative Cutter	Dennis Brookins
Production/Payroll	System One
Locations By	Filmtrucks, Inc.
Electronic Sound Effects	Electric Melody Studios
Recording Facilities	Lion's Gate Sound

Score Performed by	The Plugz:
	Tito Larriva
	Steven Hufsteter
	Charlie Quintana
	Tony Marsico

Repo Man Theme Song
Written and Performed by Iggy Pop

Coup D'Etat
Performed by the Circle Jerks
Courtesy of Lax Records

Institutionalized
Performed by Suicidal Tendencies
Courtesy of Frontier Records

TV Party
Performed by Black Flag
Courtesy of Unicorn Records

El Clavo Y La Cruz
Performed by The Plugz
Courtesy of Fatima Records

Happy Animals
Performed by Big Race

See See Rider
Performed by Louis Armstrong

Rhumboogie
Performed by the Andrew Sisters
Courtesy of MCA Records

Lite's Theme
Performed by the Juicy Bananas

Pablo Picasso
Performed by Burning Sensations
Produced by Tim McGovern

Secret Agent Man
Performed by The Plugz

I Just Want to Satisfy
Performed by the Juicy Bananas

Flor De Mal
Performed by The Plugz

Bad Man
Performed by the Juicy Bananas

When the Shit Hits the Fan
Performed by the Circle Jerks

Milk Cow Blues
Performed by Almost Famous Figures

Let's Have a War
Performed by Fear

Color by Deluxe   Prints by Technicolor

Special Thanks
NW Ayer, Inc.
Car-Freshener Corporation
Ralph's Supermarkets
Helfick Enterprises, Inc.

141

— Falling in Love (Berlin)
Sung by Merrill.
Operatic Baritone, funny.
Simpleton —

American Promise (Irving Berlin)
All Men Are Created Equal. †